I0635206

Essay on Man
Moral Essays and Satires

Alexander Pope

Contents

ESSAY ON MAN
MORAL ESSAYS
AND SATIRES

BY

Alexander Pope

AN ESSAY ON MAN.
MORAL ESSAYS AND SATIRES

BY
ALEXANDER POPE.

CASSELL & COMPANY, LIMITED:
LONDON, *PARIS & MELBOURNE*.
1891.

INTRODUCTION.

Pope's life as a writer falls into three periods, answering fairly enough to the three reigns in which he worked. Under Queen Anne he was an original poet, but made little money by his verses; under George I. he was chiefly a translator, and made much money by satisfying the French-classical taste with versions of the "Iliad" and "Odyssey." Under George I. he also edited Shakespeare, but with little profit to himself; for Shakespeare was but a Philistine in the eyes of the French-classical critics. But as the eighteenth century grew slowly to its work, signs of a deepening interest in the real issues of life distracted men's attention from the culture of the snuff-box and the fan. As Pope's genius ripened, the best part of the world in which he worked was pressing forward, as a mariner who will no longer hug the coast but crowds all sail to cross the storms of a wide unknown sea. Pope's poetry thus deepened with the course of time, and the third period of his life, which fell within the reign of George II., was that in which he produced the "Essay on Man," the "Moral Essays," and the "Satires." These deal wholly with aspects of human life and the great questions they raise, according throughout with the doctrine of the poet, and of the reasoning world about him in his latter day, that "the proper study of mankind is Man."

Wrongs in high places, and the private infamy of many who enforced the doctrines of the Church, had produced in earnest men a vigorous antagonism. Tyranny and unreason of low-minded advocates had brought religion itself into question; and profligacy of courtiers, each worshipping the golden calf seen in his mirror, had spread another form of scepticism. The intellectual scepticism, based upon an honest search for truth, could end only in making truth the surer by its questionings. The other form of scepticism, which might be traced in England from the low-minded frivolities of the court of Charles the Second, was widely spread among the weak, whose minds flinched from all earnest thought. They swelled the number of the army of bold questioners upon the ways of God to Man, but they were an idle rout of camp-followers, not combatants; they simply ate, and drank, and died.

In 1697, Pierre Bayle published at Rotterdam, his "Historical and Critical Dictionary," in which the lives of men were associated with a comment that suggested, from the ills of life, the absence of divine care in the shaping of the world. Doubt was born of the corruption of society; Nature and Man were said to be against faith in the rule of a God, wise, just, and merciful. In 1710, after Bayle's death, Leibnitz, a German philosopher then resident in Paris, wrote in French a book, with a title formed from Greek words meaning Justice of God, Theodicee, in which he met Bayle's argument by reasoning that what we cannot understand confuses us, because we see only the parts of a great whole. Bayle, he said, is now in Heaven, and from his place by the throne of God, he sees the harmony of the great Universe, and doubts no more. We see only a little part in which are many details that have purposes beyond our ken. The argument of Leibnitz's Theodicee was widely used; and although Pope said that he had never read the Theodicee, his "Essay on Man" has a like argument. When any book has a wide influence upon opinion, its general ideas pass into the minds of many people who have never read it. Many now talk about evolution and natural selection, who have never read a line of Darwin.

In the reign of George the Second, questionings did spread that went to the roots of all religious faith, and many earnest minds were busying themselves with problems of the state of Man, and of the evidence of God in the life of man, and in the course of Nature. Out of this came, nearly at the same time, two works wholly different in method and in tone--so different, that at first sight it may seem absurd to speak of them together. They were Pope's "Essay on Man," and Butler's "Analogy of Religion, Natural and Revealed, to the Constitution and Course of Nature."

Butler's "Analogy" was published in 1736; of the "Essay on Man," the first two Epistles appeared in 1732, the Third Epistle in 1733, the Fourth in 1734, and the closing Universal Hymn in 1738. It may seem even more absurd to name Pope's "Essay on Man" in the same breath with Milton's "Paradise Lost;" but to the best of his knowledge and power, in his smaller way, according to his nature and the questions of his time, Pope was, like Milton, endeavouring "to justify the ways of God to Man." He even borrowed Milton's line for his own poem, only weakening the verb, and said that he sought to "vindicate the ways of God to Man." In Milton's day the questioning all centred in the doctrine of the "Fall of Man," and questions of God's Justice were associated with debate on fate, fore-knowledge, and free will. In Pope's day the question was not theological, but went to the root of all faith in existence of a God, by declaring that the state of Man and of the world about him met such faith with an absolute denial. Pope's argument, good or bad, had nothing to do with questions of theology. Like Butler's, it sought for grounds of faith in the conditions on which doubt was rested. Milton sought to set forth the story of the Fall in such way as to show that God was love. Pope dealt with the question of God in Nature, and the world of Man.

Pope's argument was attacked with violence my M. de Crousaz, Professor of Philosophy and Mathematics in the University of Lausanne, and defended by Warburton, then chaplain to the Prince of Wales, in six letters published in 1739, and a seventh in 1740, for which Pope (who died in 1744) was deeply grateful. His offence in the eyes of de Crousaz was that he had left out of account all doctrines of orthodox theology. But if he had been orthodox of the orthodox, his argument obviously could have been directed only to the form of doubt it sought to overcome. And when his closing hymn was condemned as the freethinker's hymn, its censurers surely forgot that their arguments against it would equally apply to the Lord's Prayer, of which it is, in some degree, a paraphrase.

The first design of the Essay on Man arranged it into four books, each consisting of a distinct group of Epistles. The First Book, in four Epistles, was to treat of man in the abstract, and of his relation to the Universe. That is the whole work as we have it now. The Second Book was to treat of Man Intellectual; the Third Book, of Man Social, including ties to Church and State; the Fourth Book, of Man Moral, was to illustrate abstract truth by sketches of character. This part of the design is represented by the Moral Essays, of which four were written, to which was added, as a fifth, the Epistle to Addison which had been written much earlier, in 1715, and first published in 1720. The four Moral essays are two pairs. One pair is upon the Characters of Men and on the Characters of Women, which would have formed the opening of the subject of the Fourth Book of the Essay: the other pair shows character expressed through a right or a wrong use of Riches: in fact, Money and Morals. The four Epistles were published separately. The fourth (to the Earl of Burlington) was first published in 1731, its title then being "Of Taste;" the third (to Lord Bathurst) followed in 1732, the year of the publication of the first two Epistles on the "Essay on Man." In 1733, the year of publication of the Third Epistle of the "Essay on Man," Pope published his Moral Essay of the "Characters of Men." In 1734 followed the Fourth Epistle of the "Essay on Man;" and in 1735 the "Characters of Women," addressed to Martha Blount, the woman whom Pope loved, though he was withheld by a frail body from marriage. Thus the two works were, in fact, produced together, parts of one design.

Pope's Satires, which still deal with characters of men, followed immediately, some appearing in a folio in January, 1735. That part of the epistle to Arbuthnot forming the Prologue, which gives a character of Addison, as Atticus, had been sketched more than twelve years before, and earlier sketches of some smaller critics were introduced; but the beginning and the end, the parts in which Pope spoke of himself and of his father and mother, and his friend Dr. Arbuthnot, were written in 1733 and 1734. Then follows an imitation of the first Epistle of the Second Book of the Satires of Horace, concerning which Pope told a friend, "When I had a fever one winter in town that confined me to my room for five or six days, Lord Bolingbroke, who came to see me, happened to take up a Horace that lay on the table, and, turning it over, dropped on the first satire in the Second Book, which begins, 'Sunt, quibus in satira.' He observed how well that would suit my case if I were to imitate it in English. After he was gone, I read it over, translated it in a morning or two, and sent it to press in a week or a fortnight after" (February, 1733). "And this was the occasion of my imitating some others of the Satires and Epistles." The two dialogues finally used as the Epilogue to the Satires were first published in the year 1738, with the name of the year, "Seventeen Hundred and Thirty-eight." Samuel Johnson's "London," his first bid for recognition, appeared in the same week, and excited in Pope not admiration only, but some active endeavour to be useful to its author.

The reader of Pope, as of every author, is advised to begin by letting him say what he has to say, in his own manner to an open mind that seeks only to receive the impressions which the writer wishes to convey. First let the mind and spirit of the writer come into free, full contact with the mind and spirit of the reader, whose attitude at the first reading should be simply receptive. Such reading is the condition precedent to all true judgment of a writer's work. All criticism that is not so grounded spreads as fog over a poet's page. Read, reader, for yourself, without once pausing to remember what you have been told to think.

H.M.

POPE'S POEMS.

AN ESSAY ON MAN.
TO H. ST. JOHN LORD BOLINGBROKE.

THE DESIGN.

Having proposed to write some pieces of Human Life and Manners, such as
(to use my Lord Bacon's expression) come home to Men's Business and
Bosoms, I thought it more satisfactory to begin with considering Man in
the abstract, his Nature and his State; since, to prove any moral duty,
to enforce any moral precept, or to examine the perfection or
imperfection of any creature whatsoever, it is necessary first to know
what condition and relation it is placed in, and what is the proper end
and purpose of its being.

The science of Human Nature is, like all other sciences, reduced to a few
clear points: there are not many certain truths in this world. It is
therefore in the anatomy of the Mind as in that of the Body; more good
will accrue to mankind by attending to the large, open, and perceptible

parts, than by studying too much such finer nerves and vessels, the conformations and uses of which will for ever escape our observation. The disputes are all upon these last, and, I will venture to say, they have less sharpened the wits than the hearts of men against each other, and have diminished the practice more than advanced the theory of Morality. If I could flatter myself that this Essay has any merit, it is in steering betwixt the extremes of doctrines seemingly opposite, in passing over terms utterly unintelligible, and in forming a temperate yet not inconsistent, and a short yet not imperfect system of Ethics.

This I might have done in prose, but I chose verse, and even rhyme, for two reasons. The one will appear obvious; that principles, maxims, or precepts so written, both strike the reader more strongly at first, and are more easily retained by him afterwards: the other may seem odd, but is true, I found I could express them more shortly this way than in prose itself; and nothing is more certain, than that much of the force as well as grace of arguments or instructions depends on their conciseness. I was unable to treat this part of my subject more in detail, without becoming dry and tedious; or more poetically, without sacrificing perspicuity to ornament, without wandering from the precision, or breaking the chain of reasoning: if any man can unite all these without diminution of any of them I freely confess he will compass a thing above my capacity.

What is now published is only to be considered as a general Map of Man, marking out no more than the greater parts, their extent, their limits, and their connection, and leaving the particular to be more fully delineated in the charts which are to follow. Consequently, these Epistles in their progress (if I have health and leisure to make any progress) will be less dry, and more susceptible of poetical ornament. I am here only opening the fountains, and clearing the passage. To deduce the rivers, to follow them in their course, and to observe their effects, may be a task more agreeable. P.

ARGUMENT OF EPISTLE I.

Of the Nature and State of Man, with respect to the Universe.

Of Man in the abstract. I. That we can judge only with regard to our own system, being ignorant of the relations of systems and things, v.17, etc. II. That Man is not to be deemed imperfect, but a being suited to his place and rank in the Creation, agreeable to the general Order of Things, and conformable to Ends and Relations to him unknown, v.35, etc. III. That it is partly upon his ignorance of future events, and partly upon the hope of future state, that all his happiness in the present depends, v.77, etc. IV. The pride of aiming at more knowledge, and pretending to more Perfection, the cause of Man's error and misery. The impiety of putting himself in the place of God, and judging of the fitness or unfitness, perfection or imperfection, justice or injustice of His dispensations, v.109, etc. V. The absurdity of conceiting himself the final cause of the Creation, or expecting that perfection in the moral world, which is not in the natural, v.131, etc. VI. The unreasonableness of his complaints against Providence, while on the one hand he demands the Perfections of the Angels, and on the other the bodily qualifications of the Brutes; though to possess any of the sensitive faculties in a higher degree would render him miserable, v.173, etc. VII. That throughout the whole visible world, an universal order and gradation in the sensual and mental faculties is observed, which cause is a subordination of creature to creature, and of all creatures to Man. The gradations of sense, instinct, thought, reflection, reason; that Reason alone countervails all the other faculties, v.207. VIII. How much further this order and subordination of living creatures may extend, above and below us; were any part of which broken, not that part only, but the whole connected creation, must be destroyed, v.233. IX. The extravagance, madness, and pride of such a desire, v.250. X. The consequence of all, the absolute submission due to Providence, both as to our present and future state, v.281, etc., to the end.

EPISTLE I.

Awake, my St. John! leave all meaner things
To low ambition, and the pride of kings.
Let us (since life can little more supply
Than just to look about us and to die)
Expatiate free o'er all this scene of man;
A mighty maze! but not without a plan;
A wild, where weeds and flowers promiscuous shoot;
Or garden tempting with forbidden fruit.
Together let us beat this ample field,
Try what the open, what the covert yield;
The latent tracts, the giddy heights, explore
Of all who blindly creep, or sightless soar;
Eye Nature's walks, shoot Folly as it flies,
And catch the manners living as they rise;
Laugh where we must, be candid where we can;
But vindicate the ways of God to man.

I. Say first, of God above, or man below
What can we reason, but from what we know?
Of man, what see we but his station here,
From which to reason, or to which refer?
Through worlds unnumbered though the God be known,
'Tis ours to trace Him only in our own.
He, who through vast immensity can pierce,
See worlds on worlds compose one universe,

Observe how system into system runs,
What other planets circle other suns,
What varied being peoples every star,
May tell why Heaven has made us as we are.
But of this frame, the bearings, and the ties,
The strong connections, nice dependencies,
Gradations just, has thy pervading soul
Looked through? or can a part contain the whole?
  Is the great chain, that draws all to agree,
And drawn supports, upheld by God, or thee?

II. Presumptuous man! the reason wouldst thou find,
Why formed so weak, so little, and so blind?
First, if thou canst, the harder reason guess,
Why formed no weaker, blinder, and no less;
Ask of thy mother earth, why oaks are made
Taller or stronger than the weeds they shade?
Or ask of yonder argent fields above,
Why Jove's satellites are less than Jove?
  Of systems possible, if 'tis confest
That wisdom infinite must form the best,
Where all must full or not coherent be,
And all that rises, rise in due degree;
Then in the scale of reasoning life, 'tis plain,
There must be, somewhere, such a rank as man:
And all the question (wrangle e'er so long)
Is only this, if God has placed him wrong?
  Respecting man, whatever wrong we call,
May, must be right, as relative to all.
In human works, though laboured on with pain,
A thousand movements scarce one purpose gain;
In God's one single can its end produce;
Yet serves to second too some other use.

So man, who here seems principal alone,
Perhaps acts second to some sphere unknown,
Touches some wheel, or verges to some goal;
'Tis but a part we see, and not a whole.
　　When the proud steed shall know why man restrains
His fiery course, or drives him o'er the plains:
When the dull ox, why now he breaks the clod,
Is now a victim, and now Egypt's god:
Then shall man's pride and dulness comprehend
His actions', passions', being's, use and end;
Why doing, suffering, checked, impelled; and why
This hour a slave, the next a deity.
　　Then say not man's imperfect, Heaven in fault;
Say rather man's as perfect as he ought:
His knowledge measured to his state and place;
His time a moment, and a point his space.
If to be perfect in a certain sphere,
What matter, soon or late, or here or there?
The blest to-day is as completely so,
As who began a thousand years ago.

III. Heaven from all creatures hides the book of Fate,
All but the page prescribed, their present state:
From brutes what men, from men what spirits know:
Or who could suffer being here below?
The lamb thy riot dooms to bleed to-day,
Had he thy reason, would he skip and play?
Pleased to the last, he crops the flowery food,
And licks the hand just raised to shed his blood.
Oh, blindness to the future! kindly given,
That each may fill the circle, marked by Heaven:
Who sees with equal eye, as God of all,
A hero perish, or a sparrow fall,

Atoms or systems into ruin hurled,
And now a bubble burst, and now a world.
  Hope humbly, then; with trembling pinions soar;
Wait the great teacher Death; and God adore.
What future bliss, He gives not thee to know,
But gives that hope to be thy blessing now.
Hope springs eternal in the human breast:
Man never is, but always to be blest:
The soul, uneasy and confined from home,
Rests and expatiates in a life to come.
  Lo, the poor Indian! whose untutored mind
Sees God in clouds, or hears Him in the wind;
His soul, proud science never taught to stray
Far as the solar walk, or milky way;
Yet simple Nature to his hope has given,
Behind the cloud-topped hill, an humbler heaven;
Some safer world in depth of woods embraced,
Some happier island in the watery waste,
Where slaves once more their native land behold,
No fiends torment, no Christians thirst for gold.
To be, contents his natural desire,
He asks no angel's wing, no seraph's fire;
But thinks, admitted to that equal sky,
His faithful dog shall bear him company.

IV. Go, wiser thou! and, in thy scale of sense,
Weigh thy opinion against providence;
Call imperfection what thou fanciest such,
Say, here He gives too little, there too much;
Destroy all creatures for thy sport or gust,
Yet cry, if man's unhappy, God's unjust;
If man alone engross not Heaven's high care,
Alone made perfect here, immortal there:

Snatch from His hand the balance and the rod,
Re-judge His justice, be the God of God.
In pride, in reasoning pride, our error lies;
All quit their sphere, and rush into the skies.
Pride still is aiming at the blest abodes,
Men would be angels, angels would be gods.
Aspiring to be gods, if angels fell,
Aspiring to be angels, men rebel:
And who but wishes to invert the laws
Of order, sins against the Eternal Cause.

V. Ask for what end the heavenly bodies shine,
Earth for whose use? Pride answers, "'Tis for mine:
For me kind Nature wakes her genial power,
Suckles each herb, and spreads out every flower;
Annual for me, the grape, the rose renew
The juice nectareous, and the balmy dew;
For me, the mine a thousand treasures brings;
For me, health gushes from a thousand springs;
Seas roll to waft me, suns to light me rise;
My footstool earth, my canopy the skies."
  But errs not Nature from this gracious end,
From burning suns when livid deaths descend,
When earthquakes swallow, or when tempests sweep
Towns to one grave, whole nations to the deep?
"No, ('tis replied) the first Almighty Cause
Acts not by partial, but by general laws;
The exceptions few; some change since all began;
And what created perfect?"--Why then man?
If the great end be human happiness,
Then Nature deviates; and can man do less?
As much that end a constant course requires
Of showers and sunshine, as of man's desires;

As much eternal springs and cloudless skies,
As men for ever temperate, calm, and wise.
If plagues or earthquakes break not Heaven's design,
Why then a Borgia, or a Catiline?
Who knows but He, whose hand the lightning forms,
Who heaves old ocean, and who wings the storms;
Pours fierce ambition in a Caesar's mind,
Or turns young Ammon loose to scourge mankind?
From pride, from pride, our very reasoning springs;
Account for moral, as for natural things:
Why charge we heaven in those, in these acquit?
In both, to reason right is to submit.

   Better for us, perhaps, it might appear,
Were there all harmony, all virtue here;
That never air or ocean felt the wind;
That never passion discomposed the mind.
But all subsists by elemental strife;
And passions are the elements of life.
The general order, since the whole began,
Is kept in nature, and is kept in man.

VI. What would this man? Now upward will he soar,
And little less than angel, would be more;
Now looking downwards, just as grieved appears
To want the strength of bulls, the fur of bears
Made for his use all creatures if he call,
Say what their use, had he the powers of all?
Nature to these, without profusion, kind,
The proper organs, proper powers assigned;
Each seeming want compensated of course,
Here with degrees of swiftness, there of force;
All in exact proportion to the state;
Nothing to add, and nothing to abate.

Each beast, each insect, happy in its own:
Is Heaven unkind to man, and man alone?
Shall he alone, whom rational we call,
Be pleased with nothing, if not blessed with all?
  The bliss of man (could pride that blessing find)
Is not to act or think beyond mankind;
No powers of body or of soul to share,
But what his nature and his state can bear.
Why has not man a microscopic eye?
For this plain reason, man is not a fly.
Say what the use, were finer optics given,
To inspect a mite, not comprehend the heaven?
Or touch, if tremblingly alive all o'er,
To smart and agonize at every pore?
Or quick effluvia darting through the brain,
Die of a rose in aromatic pain?
If Nature thundered in his opening ears,
And stunned him with the music of the spheres,
How would he wish that Heaven had left him still
The whispering zephyr, and the purling rill?
Who finds not Providence all good and wise,
Alike in what it gives, and what denies?

VII. Far as Creation's ample range extends,
The scale of sensual, mental powers ascends:
Mark how it mounts, to man's imperial race,
From the green myriads in the peopled grass:
What modes of sight betwixt each wide extreme,
The mole's dim curtain, and the lynx's beam:
Of smell, the headlong lioness between,
And hound sagacious on the tainted green:
Of hearing, from the life that fills the flood,
To that which warbles through the vernal wood:

The spider's touch, how exquisitely fine!
Feels at each thread, and lives along the line:
In the nice bee, what sense so subtly true
From poisonous herbs extracts the healing dew?
How instinct varies in the grovelling swine,
Compared, half-reasoning elephant, with thine!
'Twixt that, and reason, what a nice barrier,
For ever separate, yet for ever near!
Remembrance and reflection how allayed;
What thin partitions sense from thought divide:
And middle natures, how they long to join,
Yet never passed the insuperable line!
Without this just gradation, could they be
Subjected, these to those, or all to thee?
The powers of all subdued by thee alone,
Is not thy reason all these powers in one?

VIII. See, through this air, this ocean, and this earth,
All matter quick, and bursting into birth.
Above, how high, progressive life may go!
Around, how wide! how deep extend below?
Vast chain of being! which from God began,
Natures ethereal, human, angel, man,
Beast, bird, fish, insect, what no eye can see,
No glass can reach; from Infinite to thee,
From thee to nothing. On superior powers
Were we to press, inferior might on ours:
Or in the full creation leave a void,
Where, one step broken, the great scale's destroyed:
From Nature's chain whatever link you strike,
Tenth or ten thousandth, breaks the chain alike.
    And, if each system in gradation roll
Alike essential to the amazing whole,

The least confusion but in one, not all
That system only, but the whole must fall.
Let earth unbalanced from her orbit fly,
Planets and suns run lawless through the sky;
Let ruling angels from their spheres be hurled,
Being on being wrecked, and world on world;
Heaven's whole foundations to their centre nod,
And nature tremble to the throne of God.
All this dread order break--for whom? for thee?
Vile worm!--Oh, madness! pride! impiety!

IX. What if the foot, ordained the dust to tread,
Or hand, to toil, aspired to be the head?
What if the head, the eye, or ear repined
To serve mere engines to the ruling mind?
Just as absurd for any part to claim
To be another, in this general frame:
Just as absurd, to mourn the tasks or pains,
The great directing Mind of All ordains.
   All are but parts of one stupendous whole,
Whose body Nature is, and God the soul;
That, changed through all, and yet in all the same;
Great in the earth, as in the ethereal frame;
Warms in the sun, refreshes in the breeze,
Glows in the stars, and blossoms in the trees,
Lives through all life, extends through all extent,
Spreads undivided, operates unspent;
Breathes in our soul, informs our mortal part,
As full, as perfect, in a hair as heart:
As full, as perfect, in vile man that mourns,
As the rapt seraph that adores and burns:
To him no high, no low, no great, no small;
He fills, he bounds, connects, and equals all.

X. Cease, then, nor order imperfection name:
Our proper bliss depends on what we blame.
Know thy own point: this kind, this due degree
Of blindness, weakness, Heaven bestows on thee.
Submit. In this, or any other sphere,
Secure to be as blest as thou canst bear:
Safe in the hand of one disposing Power,
Or in the natal, or the mortal hour.
All nature is but art, unknown to thee;
All chance, direction, which thou canst not see;
All discord, harmony not understood;
All partial evil, universal good:
And, spite of pride in erring reason's spite,
One truth is clear, whatever is, is right.

ARGUMENT OF EPISTLE II.

Of the Nature and State of Man with respect to Himself, as an Individual.

I. The business of Man not to pry into God, but to study himself. His Middle Nature; his Powers and Frailties, v.1 to 19. The Limits of his Capacity, v.19, etc. II. The two Principles of Man, Self-love and Reason, both necessary, v.53, etc. Self-love the stronger, and why, v.67, etc. Their end the same, v.81, etc. III. The Passions, and their use, v.93 to 130. The predominant Passion, and its force, v.132 to 160. Its Necessity, in directing Men to different purposes, v.165, etc. Its providential Use, in fixing our Principle, and ascertaining our Virtue, v.177. IV. Virtue and Vice joined in our mixed Nature; the limits near, yet the things separate and evident: What is the Office of Reason, v.202 to 216. V. How odious Vice in itself, and how we deceive ourselves into

it, v.217. VI. That, however, the Ends of Providence and general Good
are answered in our Passions and Imperfections, v.238, etc. How usefully
these are distributed to all Orders of Men, v.241. How useful they are
to Society, v.251. And to the Individuals, v.263. In every state, and
every age of life, v.273, etc.

EPISTLE II.

I. Know, then, thyself, presume not God to scan;
The proper study of mankind is man.
Placed on this isthmus of a middle state,
A being darkly wise, and rudely great:
With too much knowledge for the sceptic side,
With too much weakness for the stoic's pride,
He hangs between; in doubt to act, or rest;
In doubt to deem himself a god, or beast;
In doubt his mind or body to prefer;
Born but to die, and reasoning but to err;
Alike in ignorance, his reason such,
Whether he thinks too little, or too much:
Chaos of thought and passion, all confused;
Still by himself abused, or disabused;
Created half to rise, and half to fall;
Great lord of all things, yet a prey to all;
Sole judge of truth, in endless error hurled:
The glory, jest, and riddle of the world!
   Go, wondrous creature! mount where science guides,
Go, measure earth, weigh air, and state the tides;
Instruct the planets in what orbs to run,
Correct old time, and regulate the sun;
Go, soar with Plato to th' empyreal sphere,

To the first good, first perfect, and first fair;
Or tread the mazy round his followers trod,
And quitting sense call imitating God;
As Eastern priests in giddy circles run,
And turn their heads to imitate the sun.
Go, teach Eternal Wisdom how to rule--
Then drop into thyself, and be a fool!
   Superior beings, when of late they saw
A mortal man unfold all Nature's law,
Admired such wisdom in an earthly shape
And showed a Newton as we show an ape.
   Could he, whose rules the rapid comet bind,
Describe or fix one movement of his mind?
Who saw its fires here rise, and there descend,
Explain his own beginning, or his end?
Alas, what wonder! man's superior part
Unchecked may rise, and climb from art to art;
But when his own great work is but begun,
What reason weaves, by passion is undone.
 Trace Science, then, with Modesty thy guide;
First strip off all her equipage of pride;
Deduct what is but vanity or dress,
Or learning's luxury, or idleness;
Or tricks to show the stretch of human brain,
Mere curious pleasure, or ingenious pain;
Expunge the whole, or lop th' excrescent parts
Of all our vices have created arts;
Then see how little the remaining sum,
Which served the past, and must the times to come!

II. Two principles in human nature reign;
Self-love to urge, and reason, to restrain;
Nor this a good, nor that a bad we call,

Each works its end, to move or govern all
And to their proper operation still,
Ascribe all good; to their improper, ill.
 Self-love, the spring of motion, acts the soul;
Reason's comparing balance rules the whole.
Man, but for that, no action could attend,
And but for this, were active to no end:
Fixed like a plant on his peculiar spot,
To draw nutrition, propagate, and rot;
Or, meteor-like, flame lawless through the void,
Destroying others, by himself destroyed.
 Most strength the moving principle requires;
Active its task, it prompts, impels, inspires.
Sedate and quiet the comparing lies,
Formed but to check, deliberate, and advise.
Self-love still stronger, as its objects nigh;
Reason's at distance, and in prospect lie:
That sees immediate good by present sense;
Reason, the future and the consequence.
Thicker than arguments, temptations throng.
At best more watchful this, but that more strong.
The action of the stronger to suspend,
Reason still use, to reason still attend.
Attention, habit and experience gains;
Each strengthens reason, and self-love restrains.
 Let subtle schoolmen teach these friends to fight,
More studious to divide than to unite;
And grace and virtue, sense and reason split,
With all the rash dexterity of wit.
Wits, just like fools, at war about a name,
Have full as oft no meaning, or the same.
Self-love and reason to one end aspire,
Pain their aversion, pleasure their desire;

But greedy that, its object would devour,
This taste the honey, and not wound the flower:
Pleasure, or wrong or rightly understood,
Our greatest evil, or our greatest good.

III. Modes of self-love the passions we may call;
'Tis real good, or seeming, moves them all:
But since not every good we can divide,
And reason bids us for our own provide;
Passions, though selfish, if their means be fair,
List under Reason, and deserve her care;
Those, that imparted, court a nobler aim,
Exalt their kind, and take some virtue's name.
    In lazy apathy let stoics boast
Their virtue fixed; 'tis fixed as in a frost;
Contracted all, retiring to the breast;
But strength of mind is exercise, not rest:
The rising tempest puts in act the soul,
Parts it may ravage, but preserves the whole.
On life's vast ocean diversely we sail,
Reason the card, but passion is the gale;
Nor God alone in the still calm we find,
He mounts the storm, and walks upon the wind.
    Passions, like elements, though born to fight,
Yet, mixed and softened, in his work unite:
These, 'tis enough to temper and employ;
But what composes man, can man destroy?
Suffice that Reason keep to Nature's road,
Subject, compound them, follow her and God.
Love, hope, and joy, fair pleasure's smiling train,
Hate, fear, and grief, the family of pain,
These mixed with art, and to due bounds confined,
Make and maintain the balance of the mind;

The lights and shades, whose well-accorded strife
Gives all the strength and colour of our life.
 Pleasures are ever in our hands or eyes;
And when in act they cease, in prospect rise:
Present to grasp, and future still to find,
The whole employ of body and of mind.
All spread their charms, but charm not all alike;
On different senses different objects strike;
Hence different passions more or less inflame,
As strong or weak, the organs of the frame;
And hence once master passion in the breast,
Like Aaron's serpent, swallows up the rest.

  As man, perhaps, the moment of his breath
Receives the lurking principle of death;
The young disease that must subdue at length,
Grows with his growth, and strengthens with his strength:
So, cast and mingled with his very frame,
The mind's disease, its ruling passion came;
Each vital humour which should feed the whole,
Soon flows to this, in body and in soul:
Whatever warms the heart, or fills the head,
As the mind opens, and its functions spread,
Imagination plies her dangerous art,
And pours it all upon the peccant part.

  Nature its mother, habit is its nurse;
Wit, spirit, faculties, but make it worse;
Reason itself but gives it edge and power;
As Heaven's blest beam turns vinegar more sour.

  We, wretched subjects, though to lawful sway,
In this weak queen some favourite still obey:
Ah! if she lend not arms, as well as rules,
What can she more than tell us we are fools?
Teach us to mourn our nature, not to mend,

A sharp accuser, but a helpless friend!
Or from a judge turn pleader, to persuade
The choice we make, or justify it made;
Proud of an easy conquest all along,
She but removes weak passions for the strong;
So, when small humours gather to a gout,
The doctor fancies he has driven them out.

    Yes, Nature's road must ever be preferred;
Reason is here no guide, but still a guard:
'Tis hers to rectify, not overthrow,
And treat this passion more as friend than foe:
A mightier power the strong direction sends,
And several men impels to several ends:
Like varying winds, by other passions tossed,
This drives them constant to a certain coast.
Let power or knowledge, gold or glory, please,
Or (oft more strong than all) the love of ease;
Through life 'tis followed, even at life's expense;
The merchant's toil, the sage's indolence,
The monk's humility, the hero's pride,
All, all alike, find reason on their side.

    The eternal art, educing good from ill,
Grafts on this passion our best principle:
'Tis thus the mercury of man is fixed,
Strong grows the virtue with his nature mixed;
The dross cements what else were too refined,
And in one interest body acts with mind.

    As fruits, ungrateful to the planter's care,
On savage stocks inserted, learn to bear;
The surest virtues thus from passions shoot,
Wild nature's vigour working at the root.
What crops of wit and honesty appear
From spleen, from obstinacy, hate, or fear!

See anger, zeal and fortitude supply;
Even avarice, prudence; sloth, philosophy;
Lust, through some certain strainers well refined,
Is gentle love, and charms all womankind;
Envy, to which th' ignoble mind's a slave,
Is emulation in the learned or brave;
Nor virtue, male or female, can we name,
But what will grow on pride, or grow on shame.
　　Thus Nature gives us (let it check our pride)
The virtue nearest to our vice allied:
Reason the bias turns to good from ill
And Nero reigns a Titus, if he will.
The fiery soul abhorred in Catiline,
In Decius charms, in Curtius is divine:
The same ambition can destroy or save,
And makes a patriot as it makes a knave.
　　This light and darkness in our chaos joined,
What shall divide? The God within the mind.
　　Extremes in nature equal ends produce,
In man they join to some mysterious use;
Though each by turns the other's bound invade,
As, in some well-wrought picture, light and shade,
And oft so mix, the difference is too nice
Where ends the virtue or begins the vice.
　　Fools! who from hence into the notion fall,
That vice or virtue there is none at all.
If white and black blend, soften, and unite
A thousand ways, is there no black or white?
Ask your own heart, and nothing is so plain;
'Tis to mistake them, costs the time and pain.
　　Vice is a monster of so frightful mien,
As, to be hated, needs but to be seen;
Yet seen too oft, familiar with her face,

We first endure, then pity, then embrace.
But where th' extreme of vice, was ne'er agreed:
Ask where's the north? at York, 'tis on the Tweed;
In Scotland, at the Orcades; and there,
At Greenland, Zembla, or the Lord knows where.
No creature owns it in the first degree,
But thinks his neighbour farther gone than he;
Even those who dwell beneath its very zone,
Or never feel the rage, or never own;
What happier nations shrink at with affright,
The hard inhabitant contends is right.
  Virtuous and vicious every man must be,
Few in th' extreme, but all in the degree,
The rogue and fool by fits is fair and wise;
And even the best, by fits, what they despise.
'Tis but by parts we follow good or ill;
For, vice or virtue, self directs it still;
Each individual seeks a several goal;
But Heaven's great view is one, and that the whole.
That counter-works each folly and caprice;
That disappoints th' effect of every vice;
That, happy frailties to all ranks applied,
Shame to the virgin, to the matron pride,
Fear to the statesman, rashness to the chief,
To kings presumption, and to crowds belief:
That, virtue's ends from vanity can raise,
Which seeks no interest, no reward but praise;
And build on wants, and on defects of mind,
The joy, the peace, the glory of mankind.
  Heaven forming each on other to depend,
A master, or a servant, or a friend,
Bids each on other for assistance call,
Till one man's weakness grows the strength of all.

Wants, frailties, passions, closer still ally
The common interest, or endear the tie.
To these we owe true friendship, love sincere,
Each home-felt joy that life inherits here;
Yet from the same we learn, in its decline,
Those joys, those loves, those interests to resign;
Taught half by reason, half by mere decay,
To welcome death, and calmly pass away.
  Whate'er the passion, knowledge, fame, or pelf,
Not one will change his neighbour with himself.
The learned is happy nature to explore,
The fool is happy that he knows no more;
The rich is happy in the plenty given,
The poor contents him with the care of Heaven.
See the blind beggar dance, the cripple sing,
The sot a hero, lunatic a king;
The starving chemist in his golden views
Supremely blest, the poet in his muse.
  See some strange comfort every state attend,
And pride bestowed on all, a common friend;
See some fit passion every age supply,
Hope travels through, nor quits us when we die.
  Behold the child, by Nature's kindly law,
Pleased with a rattle, tickled with a straw:
Some livelier plaything gives his youth delight,
A little louder, but as empty quite:
Scarves, garters, gold, amuse his riper stage,
And beads and prayer-books are the toys of age:
Pleased with this bauble still, as that before;
Till tired he sleeps, and life's poor play is o'er.
  Meanwhile opinion gilds with varying rays
Those painted clouds that beautify our days;
Each want of happiness by hope supplied,

And each vacuity of sense by pride:
These build as fast as knowledge can destroy;
In folly's cup still laughs the bubble, joy;
One prospect lost, another still we gain;
And not a vanity is given in vain;
Even mean self-love becomes, by force divine,
The scale to measure others' wants by thine.
See! and confess, one comfort still must rise,
'Tis this, though man's a fool, yet God is wise.

ARGUMENT OF EPISTLE III.

Of the Nature and State of Man with respect to Society.

I. The whole Universe one system of Society, v.7, etc. Nothing made wholly for itself, nor yet wholly for another, v.27. The happiness of Animals mutual, v.49. II. Reason or Instinct operate alike to the good of each Individual, v.79. Reason or Instinct operate also to Society, in all Animals, v.109. III. How far Society carried by Instinct, v.115. How much farther by Reason, v.128. IV. Of that which is called the State of Nature, v.144. Reason instructed by Instinct in the invention of Arts, v.166, and in the Forms of Society, v.176. V. Origin of Political Societies, v.196. Origin of Monarchy, v.207. Patriarchal Government, v.212. VI. Origin of true Religion and Government, from the same principle, of Love, v.231, etc. Origin of Superstition and Tyranny, from the same principle, of Fear, v.237, etc. The Influence of Self-love operating to the social and public Good, v.266. Restoration of true Religion and Government on their first principle, v.285. Mixed Government, v.288. Various forms of each, and the true end of all, v.300, etc.

EPISTLE III.

Here, then, we rest: "The Universal Cause
Acts to one end, but acts by various laws."
In all the madness of superfluous health,
The trim of pride, the impudence of wealth,
Let this great truth be present night and day;
But most be present, if we preach or pray.
   Look round our world; behold the chain of love
Combining all below and all above.
See plastic Nature working to this end,
The single atoms each to other tend,
Attract, attracted to, the next in place
Formed and impelled its neighbour to embrace.
See matter next, with various life endued,
Press to one centre still, the general good.
See dying vegetables life sustain,
See life dissolving vegetate again:
All forms that perish other forms supply
(By turns we catch the vital breath, and die),
Like bubbles on the sea of matter borne,
They rise, they break, and to that sea return.
Nothing is foreign: parts relate to whole;
One all-extending, all-preserving soul
Connects each being, greatest with the least;
Made beast in aid of man, and man of beast;
All served, all serving: nothing stands alone;
The chain holds on, and where it ends, unknown.
   Has God, thou fool! worked solely for thy Thy good,
Thy joy, thy pastime, thy attire, thy food?
Who for thy table feeds the wanton fawn,

For him as kindly spread the flowery lawn:
Is it for thee the lark ascends and sings?
Joy tunes his voice, joy elevates his wings.
Is it for thee the linnet pours his throat?
Loves of his own and raptures swell the note.
The bounding steed you pompously bestride,
Shares with his lord the pleasure and the pride.
Is thine alone the seed that strews the plain?
The birds of heaven shall vindicate their grain.
Thine the full harvest of the golden year?
Part pays, and justly, the deserving steer:
The hog, that ploughs not nor obeys thy call,
Lives on the labours of this lord of all.

   Know, Nature's children all divide her care;
The fur that warms a monarch, warmed a bear.
While man exclaims, "See all things for my use!"
"See man for mine!" replies a pampered goose:
And just as short of reason he must fall,
Who thinks all made for one, not one for all.

   Grant that the powerful still the weak control;
Be man the wit and tyrant of the whole:
Nature that tyrant checks; he only knows,
And helps, another creature's wants and woes.
Say, will the falcon, stooping from above,
Smit with her varying plumage, spare the dove?
Admires the jay the insect's gilded wings?
Or hears the hawk when Philomela sings?
Man cares for all: to birds he gives his woods,
To beasts his pastures, and to fish his floods;
For some his interest prompts him to provide,
For more his pleasure, yet for more his pride:
All feed on one vain patron, and enjoy
The extensive blessing of his luxury.

That very life his learned hunger craves,
He saves from famine, from the savage saves;
Nay, feasts the animal he dooms his feast,
And, till he ends the being, makes it blest;
Which sees no more the stroke, or feels the pain,
Than favoured man by touch ethereal slain.
The creature had his feast of life before;
Thou too must perish when thy feast is o'er!
  To each unthinking being, Heaven, a friend,
Gives not the useless knowledge of its end:
To man imparts it; but with such a view
As, while he dreads it, makes him hope it too;
The hour concealed, and so remote the fear,
Death still draws nearer, never seeming near.
Great standing miracle! that Heaven assigned
Its only thinking thing this turn of mind.

II. Whether with reason, or with instinct blest,
Know, all enjoy that power which suits them best;
To bliss alike by that direction tend,
And find the means proportioned to their end.
Say, where full instinct is the unerring guide,
What pope or council can they need beside?
Reason, however able, cool at best,
Cares not for service, or but serves when pressed,
Stays till we call, and then not often near;
But honest instinct comes a volunteer,
Sure never to o'er-shoot, but just to hit;
While still too wide or short is human wit;
Sure by quick nature happiness to gain,
Which heavier reason labours at in vain,
This too serves always, reason never long;
One must go right, the other may go wrong.

See then the acting and comparing powers
One in their nature, which are two in ours;
And reason raise o'er instinct as you can,
In this 'tis God directs, in that 'tis man.
  Who taught the nations of the field and wood
To shun their poison, and to choose their food?
Prescient, the tides or tempests to withstand,
Build on the wave, or arch beneath the sand?
Who made the spider parallels design,
Sure as Demoivre, without rule or line?
Who did the stork, Columbus-like, explore
Heavens not his own, and worlds unknown before?
Who calls the council, states the certain day,
Who forms the phalanx, and who points the way?

III. God in the nature of each being founds
Its proper bliss, and sets its proper bounds:
But as He framed a whole, the whole to bless,
On mutual wants built mutual happiness:
So from the first, eternal order ran,
And creature linked to creature, man to man.
Whate'er of life all-quickening ether keeps,
Or breathes through air, or shoots beneath the deeps,
Or pours profuse on earth, one nature feeds
The vital flame, and swells the genial seeds.
Not man alone, but all that roam the wood,
Or wing the sky, or roll along the flood,
Each loves itself, but not itself alone,
Each sex desires alike, till two are one.
Nor ends the pleasure with the fierce embrace;
They love themselves, a third time, in their race.
Thus beast and bird their common charge attend,
The mothers nurse it, and the sires defend;

The young dismissed to wander earth or air,
There stops the instinct, and there ends the care;
The link dissolves, each seeks a fresh embrace,
Another love succeeds, another race.
A longer care man's helpless kind demands;
That longer care contracts more lasting bands:
Reflection, reason, still the ties improve,
At once extend the interest and the love;
With choice we fix, with sympathy we burn;
Each virtue in each passion takes its turn;
And still new needs, new helps, new habits rise.
That graft benevolence on charities.
Still as one brood, and as another rose,
These natural love maintained, habitual those.
The last, scarce ripened into perfect man,
Saw helpless him from whom their life began:
Memory and forecast just returns engage,
That pointed back to youth, this on to age;
While pleasure, gratitude, and hope combined,
Still spread the interest, and preserved the kind.

IV. Nor think, in Nature's state they blindly trod;
The state of nature was the reign of God:
Self-love and social at her birth began,
Union the bond of all things, and of man.
Pride then was not; nor arts, that pride to aid;
Man walked with beast, joint tenant of the shade;
The same his table, and the same his bed;
No murder clothed him, and no murder fed.
In the same temple, the resounding wood,
All vocal beings hymned their equal God:
The shrine with gore unstained, with gold undressed,
Unbribed, unbloody, stood the blameless priest:

Heaven's attribute was universal care,
And man's prerogative to rule, but spare.
Ah! how unlike the man of times to come!
Of half that live the butcher and the tomb;
Who, foe to nature, hears the general groan,
Murders their species, and betrays his own.
But just disease to luxury succeeds,
And every death its own avenger breeds;
The fury-passions from that blood began,
And turned on man a fiercer savage, man.
  See him from Nature rising slow to art!
To copy instinct then was reason's part;
Thus then to man the voice of Nature spake--
"Go, from the creatures thy instructions take:
Learn from the birds what food the thickets yield;
Learn from the beasts the physic of the field;
Thy arts of building from the bee receive;
Learn of the mole to plough, the worm to weave;
Learn of the little nautilus to sail,
Spread the thin oar, and catch the driving gale.
Here too all forms of social union find,
And hence let reason, late, instruct mankind:
Here subterranean works and cities see;
There towns aerial on the waving tree.
Learn each small people's genius, policies,
The ant's republic, and the realm of bees;
How those in common all their wealth bestow,
And anarchy without confusion know;
And these for ever, though a monarch reign,
Their separate cells and properties maintain.
Mark what unvaried laws preserve each state,
Laws wise as nature, and as fixed as fate.
In vain thy reason finer webs shall draw,

Entangle justice in her net of law,
And right, too rigid, harden into wrong;
Still for the strong too weak, the weak too strong.
Yet go! and thus o'er all the creatures sway,
Thus let the wiser make the rest obey;
And, for those arts mere instinct could afford,
Be crowned as monarchs, or as gods adored."

V. Great Nature spoke; observant men obeyed;
Cities were built, societies were made:
Here rose one little state: another near
Grew by like means, and joined, through love or fear.
Did here the trees with ruddier burdens bend,
And there the streams in purer rills descend?
What war could ravish, commerce could bestow,
And he returned a friend, who came a foe.
Converse and love mankind might strongly draw,
When love was liberty, and Nature law.
Thus States were formed; the name of king unknown,
'Till common interest placed the sway in one.
'Twas virtue only (or in arts or arms,
Diffusing blessings, or averting harms)
The same which in a sire the sons obeyed,
A prince the father of a people made.

VI. Till then, by Nature crowned, each patriarch sate,
King, priest, and parent of his growing state;
On him, their second providence, they hung,
Their law his eye, their oracle his tongue.
He from the wondering furrow called the food,
Taught to command the fire, control the flood,
Draw forth the monsters of the abyss profound,
Or fetch the aerial eagle to the ground.

Till drooping, sickening, dying they began
Whom they revered as God to mourn as man:
Then, looking up, from sire to sire, explored
One great first Father, and that first adored.
Or plain tradition that this all begun,
Conveyed unbroken faith from sire to son;
The worker from the work distinct was known,
And simple reason never sought but one:
Ere wit oblique had broke that steady light,
Man, like his Maker, saw that all was right;
To virtue, in the paths of pleasure, trod,
And owned a Father when he owned a God.
Love all the faith, and all the allegiance then;
For Nature knew no right divine in men,
No ill could fear in God; and understood
A sovereign being but a sovereign good.
True faith, true policy, united ran,
This was but love of God, and this of man.
   Who first taught souls enslaved, and realms undone,
The enormous faith of many made for one;
That proud exception to all Nature's laws,
To invert the world, and counter-work its cause?
Force first made conquest, and that conquest, law;
Till superstition taught the tyrant awe,
Then shared the tyranny, then lent it aid,
And gods of conquerors, slaves of subjects made:
She, 'midst the lightning's blaze, and thunder's sound,
When rocked the mountains, and when groaned the ground,
She taught the weak to bend, the proud to pray,
To power unseen, and mightier far than they:
She, from the rending earth and bursting skies,
Saw gods descend, and fiends infernal rise:
Here fixed the dreadful, there the blest abodes;

Fear made her devils, and weak hope her gods;
Gods partial, changeful, passionate, unjust,
Whose attributes were rage, revenge, or lust;
Such as the souls of cowards might conceive,
And, formed like tyrants, tyrants would believe.
Zeal then, not charity, became the guide;
And hell was built on spite, and heaven on pride,
Then sacred seemed the ethereal vault no more;
Altars grew marble then, and reeked with gore;
Then first the flamen tasted living food;
Next his grim idol smeared with human blood;
With heaven's own thunders shook the world below,
And played the god an engine on his foe.
  So drives self-love, through just and through unjust,
To one man's power, ambition, lucre, lust:
The same self-love, in all, becomes the cause
Of what restrains him, government and laws.
For, what one likes if others like as well,
What serves one will when many wills rebel?
How shall he keep, what, sleeping or awake,
A weaker may surprise, a stronger take?
His safety must his liberty restrain:
All join to guard what each desires to gain.
Forced into virtue thus by self-defence,
Even kings learned justice and benevolence:
Self-love forsook the path it first pursued,
And found the private in the public good.
  'Twas then, the studious head or generous mind,
Follower of God, or friend of human-kind,
Poet or patriot, rose but to restore
The faith and moral Nature gave before;
Re-lumed her ancient light, not kindled new;
If not God's image, yet His shadow drew:

Taught power's due use to people and to kings,
Taught nor to slack, nor strain its tender strings,
The less, or greater, set so justly true,
That touching one must strike the other too;
Till jarring interests, of themselves create
The according music of a well-mixed state.
Such is the world's great harmony, that springs
From order, union, full consent of things:
Where small and great, where weak and mighty, made
To serve, not suffer, strengthen, not invade;
More powerful each as needful to the rest,
And, in proportion as it blesses, blest;
Draw to one point, and to one centre bring
Beast, man, or angel, servant, lord, or king.

   For forms of government let fools contest;
Whate'er is best administered is best:
For modes of faith let graceless zealots fight;
His can't be wrong whose life is in the right:
In faith and hope the world will disagree,
But all mankind's concern is charity:
All must be false that thwart this one great end;
And all of God, that bless mankind or mend.

   Man, like the generous vine, supported lives;
The strength he gains is from the embrace he gives.
On their own axis as the planets run,
Yet make at once their circle round the sun;
So two consistent motions act the soul;
And one regards itself, and one the whole.

   Thus God and Nature linked the general frame,
And bade self-love and social be the same.

ARGUMENT OF EPISTLE IV.

Of the Nature and State of Man with respect to Happiness.

I. False Notions of Happiness, Philosophical and Popular, answered from v.19 to 77. II. It is the End of all Men, and attainable by all, v.30. God intends Happiness to be equal; and to be so, it must be social, since all particular Happiness depends on general, and since He governs by general, not particular Laws, v.37. As it is necessary for Order, and the peace and welfare of Society, that external goods should be unequal, Happiness is not made to consist in these, v.51. But, notwithstanding that inequality, the balance of Happiness among Mankind is kept even by Providence, by the two Passions of Hope and Fear, v.70. III. What the Happiness of Individuals is, as far as is consistent with the constitution of this world; and that the good Man has here the advantage, V.77. The error of imputing to Virtue what are only the calamities of Nature or of Fortune, v.94. IV. The folly of expecting that God should alter His general Laws in favour of particulars, v.121. V. That we are not judges who are good; but that, whoever they are, they must be happiest, v.133, etc. VI. That external goods are not the proper rewards, but often inconsistent with, or destructive of Virtue, v.165. That even these can make no Man happy without Virtue: Instanced in Riches, v.183. Honours, v.191. Nobility, v.203. Greatness, v.215. Fame, v.235. Superior Talents, v.257, etc. With pictures of human Infelicity in Men possessed of them all, v.267, etc. VII. That Virtue only constitutes a Happiness, whose object is universal, and whose prospect eternal, v.307, etc. That the perfection of Virtue and Happiness consists in a conformity to the Order of Providence here, and a Resignation to it here and hereafter, v.326, etc.

EPISTLE IV.

Oh, happiness, our being's end and aim!
Good, pleasure, ease, content! whate'er thy name:
That something still which prompts the eternal sigh,
For which we bear to live, or dare to die,
Which still so near us, yet beyond us lies,
O'erlooked, seen double, by the fool, and wise.
Plant of celestial seed! if dropped below,
Say, in what mortal soil thou deign'st to grow?
Fair opening to some Court's propitious shine,
Or deep with diamonds in the flaming mine?
Twined with the wreaths Parnassian laurels yield,
Or reaped in iron harvests of the field?
Where grows?--where grows it not? If vain our toil,
We ought to blame the culture, not the soil:
Fixed to no spot is happiness sincere,
'Tis nowhere to be found, or everywhere;
'Tis never to be bought, but always free,
And fled from monarchs, St. John! dwells with thee.
  Ask of the learned the way? The learned are blind;
This bids to serve, and that to shun mankind;
Some place the bliss in action, some in ease,
Those call it pleasure, and contentment these;
Some, sunk to beasts, find pleasure end in pain;
Some, swelled to gods, confess even virtue vain;
Or indolent, to each extreme they fall,
To trust in everything, or doubt of all.
  Who thus define it, say they more or less
Than this, that happiness is happiness?
  Take Nature's path, and mad opinions leave;

All states can reach it, and all heads conceive;
Obvious her goods, in no extreme they dwell;
There needs but thinking right, and meaning well;
And mourn our various portions as we please,
Equal is common sense, and common ease.
  Remember, man, "the Universal Cause
Acts not by partial, but by general laws;"
And makes what happiness we justly call
Subsist not in the good of one, but all.
There's not a blessing individuals find,
But some way leans and hearkens to the kind:
No bandit fierce, no tyrant mad with pride,
No caverned hermit, rests self-satisfied:
Who most to shun or hate mankind pretend,
Seek an admirer, or would fix a friend:
Abstract what others feel, what others think,
All pleasures sicken, and all glories sink:
Each has his share; and who would more obtain,
Shall find, the pleasure pays not half the pain.
  Order is Heaven's first law; and this confest,
Some are, and must be, greater than the rest,
More rich, more wise; but who infers from hence
That such are happier, shocks all common sense.
Heaven to mankind impartial we confess,
If all are equal in their happiness:
But mutual wants this happiness increase;
All Nature's difference keeps all Nature's peace.
Condition, circumstance is not the thing;
Bliss is the same in subject or in king,
In who obtain defence, or who defend,
In him who is, or him who finds a friend:
Heaven breathes through every member of the whole
One common blessing, as one common soul.

But fortune's gifts if each alike possessed,
And each were equal, must not all contest?
If then to all men happiness was meant,
God in externals could not place content.

  Fortune her gifts may variously dispose,
And these be happy called, unhappy those;
But Heaven's just balance equal will appear,
While those are placed in hope, and these in fear:
Nor present good or ill, the joy or curse,
But future views of better or of worse,

  Oh, sons of earth! attempt ye still to rise,
By mountains piled on mountains, to the skies,
Heaven still with laughter the vain toil surveys,
And buries madmen in the heaps they raise.

  Know, all the good that individuals find,
Or God and Nature meant to mere mankind,
Reason's whole pleasure, all the joys of sense,
Lie in three words, health, peace, and competence.
But health consists with temperance alone;
And peace, oh, virtue! peace is all thy own.
The good or bad the gifts of fortune gain;
But these less taste them, as they worse obtain.
Say, in pursuit of profit or delight,
Who risk the most, that take wrong means, or right;
Of vice or virtue, whether blessed or cursed,
Which meets contempt, or which compassion first?
Count all the advantage prosperous vice attains,
'Tis but what virtue flies from and disdains:
And grant the bad what happiness they would,
One they must want, which is, to pass for good.

  Oh, blind to truth, and God's whole scheme below,
Who fancy bliss to vice, to virtue woe!
Who sees and follows that great scheme the best,

Best knows the blessing, and will most be blest.
But fools the good alone unhappy call,
For ills or accidents that chance to all.
See Falkland dies, the virtuous and the just!
See god-like Turenne prostrate on the dust!
See Sidney bleeds amid the martial strife!
Was this their virtue, or contempt of life?
Say, was it virtue, more though Heaven ne'er gave,
Lamented Digby! sunk thee to the grave?
Tell me, if virtue made the son expire,
Why, full of days and honour, lives the sire?
Why drew Marseilles' good bishop purer breath,
When Nature sickened, and each gale was death?
Or why so long (in life if long can be)
Lent Heaven a parent to the poor and me?
  What makes all physical or moral ill?
There deviates Nature, and here wanders will.
God sends not ill; if rightly understood,
Or partial ill is universal good,
Or change admits, or Nature lets it fall;
Short, and but rare, till man improved it all.
We just as wisely might of Heaven complain
That righteous Abel was destroyed by Cain,
As that the virtuous son is ill at ease
When his lewd father gave the dire disease.
Think we, like some weak prince, the Eternal Cause
Prone for His favourites to reverse His laws?
  Shall burning Etna, if a sage requires,
Forget to thunder, and recall her fires?
On air or sea new motions be imprest,
Oh, blameless Bethel! to relieve thy breast?
When the loose mountain trembles from on high,
Shall gravitation cease, if you go by?

Or some old temple, nodding to its fall,
For Chartres' head reserve the hanging wall?
  But still this world (so fitted for the knave)
Contents us not. A better shall we have?
A kingdom of the just then let it be:
But first consider how those just agree.
The good must merit God's peculiar care:
But who, but God, can tell us who they are?
One thinks on Calvin Heaven's own spirit fell;
Another deems him instrument of hell;
If Calvin feel Heaven's blessing, or its rod.
This cries there is, and that, there is no God.
What shocks one part will edify the rest,
Nor with one system can they all be blest.
The very best will variously incline,
And what rewards your virtue, punish mine.
Whatever is, is right. This world, 'tis true,
Was made for Caesar--but for Titus too:
And which more blest? who chained his country, say,
Or he whose virtue sighed to lose a day?
  "But sometimes virtue starves, while vice is fed."
What then? Is the reward of virtue bread?
That, vice may merit, 'tis the price of toil;
The knave deserves it, when he tills the soil,
The knave deserves it, when he tempts the main,
Where folly fights for kings, or dives for gain.
The good man may be weak, be indolent;
Nor is his claim to plenty, but content.
But grant him riches, your demand is o'er?
"No--shall the good want health, the good want power?"
Add health, and power, and every earthly thing,
"Why bounded power? why private? why no king?"
Nay, why external for internal given?

Why is not man a god, and earth a heaven?
Who ask and reason thus, will scarce conceive
God gives enough, while He has more to give:
Immense the power, immense were the demand;
Say, at what part of nature will they stand?
   What nothing earthly gives, or can destroy,
The soul's calm sunshine, and the heartfelt joy,
Is virtue's prize: A better would you fix?
Then give humility a coach and six,
Justice a conqueror's sword, or truth a gown,
Or public spirit its great cure, a crown.
Weak, foolish man! will heaven reward us there
With the same trash mad mortals wish for here?
The boy and man an individual makes,
Yet sighest thou now for apples and for cakes?
Go, like the Indian, in another life
Expect thy dog, thy bottle, and thy wife:
As well as dream such trifles are assigned,
As toys and empires, for a God-like mind.
Rewards, that either would to virtue bring
No joy, or be destructive of the thing:
How oft by these at sixty are undone
The virtues of a saint at twenty-one!
To whom can riches give repute or trust,
Content, or pleasure, but the good and just?
Judges and senates have been bought for gold,
Esteem and love were never to be sold.
Oh, fool! to think God hates the worthy mind,
The lover and the love of human kind,
Whose life is healthful, and whose conscience clear,
Because he wants a thousand pounds a year.
   Honour and shame from no condition rise;
Act well your part, there all the honour lies.

Fortune in men has some small difference made,
One flaunts in rags, one flutters in brocade;
The cobbler aproned, and the parson gowned,
The friar hooded, and the monarch crowned,
"What differ more (you cry) than crown and cowl?"
I'll tell you, friend! a wise man and a fool.
You'll find, if once the monarch acts the monk,
Or, cobbler-like, the parson will be drunk,
Worth makes the man, and want of it, the fellow;
The rest is all but leather or prunella.

    Stuck o'er with titles and hung round with strings,
That thou mayest be by kings, or wh***s of kings.
Boast the pure blood of an illustrious race,
In quiet flow from Lucrece to Lucrece;
But by your fathers' worth if yours you rate,
Count me those only who were good and great.
Go! if your ancient, but ignoble blood
Has crept through scoundrels ever since the flood,
Go! and pretend your family is young;
Nor own, your fathers have been fools so long.
What can ennoble sots, or slaves, or cowards?
Alas! not all the blood of all the Howards.

    Look next on greatness; say where greatness lies?
"Where, but among the heroes and the wise?"
Heroes are much the same, the points agreed,
From Macedonia's madman to the Swede;
The whole strange purpose of their lives, to find
Or make, an enemy of all mankind?
Not one looks backward, onward still he goes,
Yet ne'er looks forward farther than his nose.
No less alike the politic and wise;
All sly slow things, with circumspective eyes;
Men in their loose unguarded hours they take,

Not that themselves are wise, but others weak.
But grant that those can conquer, these can cheat;
'Tis phrase absurd to call a villain great:
Who wickedly is wise, or madly brave,
Is but the more a fool, the more a knave.
Who noble ends by noble means obtains,
Or failing, smiles in exile or in chains,
Like good Aurelius let him reign, or bleed
Like Socrates, that man is great indeed.
  What's fame? a fancied life in others' breath,
A thing beyond us, even before our death.
Just what you hear, you have, and what's unknown
The same (my Lord) if Tully's, or your own.
All that we feel of it begins and ends
In the small circle of our foes or friends;
To all beside as much an empty shade
An Eugene living, as a Caesar dead;
Alike or when, or where, they shone, or shine,
Or on the Rubicon, or on the Rhine.
A wit's a feather, and a chief a rod;
An honest man's the noblest work of God.
Fame but from death a villain's name can save,
As justice tears his body from the grave;
When what the oblivion better were resigned,
Is hung on high, to poison half mankind.
All fame is foreign, but of true desert;
Plays round the head, but comes not to the heart:
One self-approving hour whole years outweighs
Of stupid starers, and of loud huzzas;
And more true joy Marcellus exiled feels,
Than Caesar with a senate at his heels.
  In parts superior what advantage lies?
Tell (for you can) what is it to be wise?

'Tis but to know how little can be known;
To see all others' faults, and feel our own;
Condemned in business or in arts to drudge,
Without a second or without a judge;
Truths would you teach or save a sinking land,
All fear, none aid you, and few understand.
Painful pre-eminence! yourself to view
Above life's weakness, and its comforts too.
  Bring, then, these blessings to a strict account;
Make fair deductions; see to what they mount;
How much of other each is sure to cost;
How each for other oft is wholly lost;
How inconsistent greater goods with these;
How sometimes life is risked, and always ease;
Think, and if still the things thy envy call,
Say, would'st thou be the man to whom they fall?
To sigh for ribands if thou art so silly,
Mark how they grace Lord Umbra, or Sir Billy:
Is yellow dirt the passion of thy life?
Look but on Gripus, or on Gripus' wife;
If parts allure thee, think how Bacon shined,
The wisest, brightest, meanest of mankind:
Or ravished with the whistling of a name,
See Cromwell; damned to everlasting fame!
If all, united, thy ambition call,
From ancient story learn to scorn them all.
There, in the rich, the honoured, famed, and great,
See the false scale of happiness complete!
In hearts of kings, or arms of queens who lay,
How happy! those to ruin, these betray.
Mark by what wretched steps their glory grows,
From dirt and seaweed as proud Venice rose;
In each how guilt and greatness equal ran,

And all that raised the hero, sunk the man:
Now Europe's laurels on their brows behold,
But stained with blood, or ill exchanged for gold;
Then see them broke with toils or sunk with ease,
Or infamous for plundered provinces.
Oh, wealth ill-fated! which no act of fame
E'er taught to shine, or sanctified from shame;
What greater bliss attends their close of life?
Some greedy minion, or imperious wife.
The trophied arches, storeyed halls invade
And haunt their slumbers in the pompous shade.
Alas! not dazzled with their noontide ray,
Compute the morn and evening to the day;
The whole amount of that enormous fame,
A tale, that blends their glory with their shame;
   Know, then, this truth (enough for man to know)
"Virtue alone is happiness below."
The only point where human bliss stands still,
And tastes the good without the fall to ill;
Where only merit constant pay receives,
Is blest in what it takes, and what it gives;
The joy unequalled, if its end it gain,
And if it lose, attended with no pain;
Without satiety, though e'er so blessed,
And but more relished as the more distressed:
The broadest mirth unfeeling folly wears,
Less pleasing far than virtue's very tears:
Good, from each object, from each place acquired
For ever exercised, yet never tired;
Never elated, while one man's oppressed;
Never dejected while another's blessed;
And where no wants, no wishes can remain,
Since but to wish more virtue, is to gain.

See the sole bliss Heaven could on all bestow!
Which who but feels can taste, but thinks can know:
Yet poor with fortune, and with learning blind,
The bad must miss; the good, untaught, will find;
Slave to no sect, who takes no private road,
But looks through Nature up to Nature's God;
Pursues that chain which links the immense design,
Joins heaven and earth, and mortal and divine;
Sees, that no being any bliss can know,
But touches some above, and some below;
Learns, from this union of the rising whole,
The first, last purpose of the human soul;
And knows, where faith, law, morals, all began,
All end, in love of God, and love of man.

  For Him alone, hope leads from goal to goal,
And opens still, and opens on his soul!
Till lengthened on to faith, and unconfined,
It pours the bliss that fills up all the mind
He sees, why Nature plants in man alone
Hope of known bliss, and faith in bliss unknown:
(Nature, whose dictates to no other kind
Are given in vain, but what they seek they find)
Wise is her present; she connects in this
His greatest virtue with his greatest bliss;
At once his own bright prospect to be blest,
And strongest motive to assist the rest.

  Self-love thus pushed to social, to divine,
Gives thee to make thy neighbour's blessing thine.
Is this too little for the boundless heart?
Extend it, let thy enemies have part:
Grasp the whole worlds of reason, life, and sense,
In one close system of benevolence:
Happier as kinder, in whate'er degree,

And height of bliss but height of charity.
  God loves from whole to parts: but human soul
Must rise from individual to the whole.
Self-love but serves the virtuous mind to wake,
As the small pebble stirs the peaceful lake!
The centre moved, a circle straight succeeds,
Another still, and still another spreads;
Friend, parent, neighbour, first it will embrace;
His country next; and next all human race;
Wide and more wide, the o'erflowings of the mind
Take every creature in, of every kind;
Earth smiles around, with boundless bounty blest,
And Heaven beholds its image in his breast.
  Come, then, my friend! my genius! come along;
Oh, master of the poet, and the song!
And while the muse now stoops, or now ascends,
To man's low passions, or their glorious ends,
Teach me, like thee, in various nature wise,
To fall with dignity, with temper rise;
Formed by thy converse, happily to steer
From grave to gay, from lively to severe;
Correct with spirit, eloquent with ease,
Intent to reason, or polite to please.
Oh! while along the stream of time thy name
Expanded flies, and gathers all its fame,
Say, shall my little bark attendant sail,
Pursue the triumph, and partake the gale?
When statesmen, heroes, kings, in dust repose,
Whose sons shall blush their fathers were thy foes,
Shall then this verse to future age pretend
Thou wert my guide, philosopher, and friend?
That urged by thee, I turned the tuneful art
From sounds to things, from fancy to the heart;

From wit's false mirror held up Nature's light;
Showed erring pride, whatever is, is right;
That reason, passion, answer one great aim;
That true self-love and social are the same;
That virtue only makes our bliss below;
And all our knowledge is, ourselves to know.

THE UNIVERSAL PRAYER.
DEO OPT. MAX.

Father of all! in every age,
   In every clime adored,
By saint, by savage, and by sage,
   Jehovah, Jove, or Lord!

Thou Great First Cause, least understood,
   Who all my sense confined
To know but this, that Thou art good,
   And that myself am blind;

Yet gave me, in this dark estate,
   To see the good from ill;
And binding Nature fast in fate,
   Left free the human will.

What conscience dictates to be done,
   Or warns me not to do,
This, teach me more than Hell to shun,
   That, more than Heaven pursue.

What blessings Thy free bounty gives,
  Let me not cast away;
For God is paid when man receives,
  To enjoy is to obey.

Yet not to earth's contracted span
  Thy goodness let me bound,
Or think Thee Lord alone of man,
  When thousand worlds are round:

Let not this weak, unknowing hand
  Presume Thy bolts to throw,
And deal damnation round the land,
  On each I judge Thy foe.

If I am right, Thy grace impart,
  Still in the right to stay;
If I am wrong, oh, teach my heart
  To find that better way.

Save me alike from foolish pride,
  Or impious discontent,
At aught Thy wisdom has denied,
  Or aught Thy goodness lent.

Teach me to feel another's woe,
  To hide the fault I see;
That mercy I to others show,
  That mercy show to me.

Mean though I am, not wholly so,
  Since quickened by Thy breath;

Oh, lead me wheresoe'er I go,
   Through this day's life or death.

This day, be bread and peace my lot:
   All else beneath the sun,
Thou know'st if best bestowed or not;
   And let Thy will be done.

To Thee, whose temple is all space,
   Whose altar earth, sea, skies,
One chorus let all being raise,
   All Nature's incense rise!

MORAL ESSAYS,
IN FOUR EPISTLES TO SEVERAL PERSONS.

Est brevitate opus, ut currat sententia, neu se
Impediat verbis lassas onerantibus aures:
Et sermone opus est modo tristi, saepe jocoso,
Defendente vicem modo Rhetoris atque Poetae,
Interdum urbani, parcentis viribus, atque
Extenuantis eas consulto.--HOR. (Sat. I. X. 9-14.)

EPISTLE I. TO SIR RICHARD TEMPLE, LORD COBHAM.

ARGUMENT.

Of the Knowledge and Characters of Men.

I. That it is not sufficient for this knowledge to consider Man in the Abstract: Books will not serve the purpose, nor yet our own Experience singly, v.1. General maxims, unless they be formed upon both, will be but notional, v.10. Some Peculiarity in every man, characteristic to himself, yet varying from himself, v.15. Difficulties arising from our own Passions, Fancies, Faculties, etc., v.31. The shortness of Life, to observe in, and the uncertainty of the Principles of action in men, to observe by, v.37, etc. Our own Principle of action often hid from ourselves, v.41. Some few Characters plain, but in general confounded, dissembled, or inconsistent, v.51. The same man utterly different in different places and seasons, v.71. Unimaginable weaknesses in the greatest, v.70, etc. Nothing constant and certain but God and Nature, v.95. No judging of the Motives from the actions; the same actions proceeding from contrary Motives, and the same Motives influencing contrary actions v.100. II. Yet to form Characters, we can only take the strongest actions of a man's life, and try to make them agree: The utter uncertainty of this, from Nature itself, and from Policy, v.120. Characters given according to the rank of men of the world, v.135. And some reason for it, v.140. Education alters the Nature, or at least Character of many, v.149. Actions, Passions, Opinions, Manners, Hu-

mours,
or Principles all subject to change. No judging by Nature, from v.158 to
178. III. It only remains to find (if we can) his Ruling Passion: That
will certainly influence all the rest, and can reconcile the seeming or
real inconsistency of all his actions, v.175. Instanced in the
extraordinary character of Clodio, v.179. A caution against mistaking
second qualities for first, which will destroy all possibility of the
knowledge of mankind, v.210. Examples of the strength of the Ruling
Passion, and its continuation to the last breath, v.222, etc.

Yes, you despise the man to books confined,
Who from his study rails at human kind;
Though what he learns he speaks, and may advance
Some general maxims, or be right by chance.
The coxcomb bird, so talkative and grave,
That from his cage cries c**d, w**e, and knave,
Though many a passenger he rightly call,
You hold him no philosopher at all.
   And yet the fate of all extremes is such,
Men may be read as well as books, too much.
To observations which ourselves we make,
We grow more partial for the observer's sake;
To written wisdom, as another's, less:
Maxims are drawn from notions, those from guess.
There's some peculiar in each leaf and grain,
Some unmarked fibre, or some varying vein:
Shall only man be taken in the gross?
Grant but as many sorts of mind as moss.
   That each from other differs, first confess;
Next, that he varies from himself no less:
Add Nature's, custom's reason's passion's strife,
And all opinion's colours cast on life.
   Our depths who fathoms, or our shallows finds,

Quick whirls, and shifting eddies, of our minds?
On human actions reason though you can,
It may be reason, but it is not man:
His principle of action once explore,
That instant 'tis his principle no more.
Like following life through creatures you dissect,
You lose it in the moment you detect.
   Yet more; the difference is as great between
The optics seeing, as the object seen.
All manners take a tincture from our own;
Or come discoloured through our passions shown.
Or fancy's beam enlarges, multiplies,
Contracts, inverts, and gives ten thousand dyes.
   Nor will life's stream for observation stay,
It hurries all too fast to mark their way:
In vain sedate reflections we would make,
When half our knowledge we must snatch, not take.
Oft, in the passion's wild rotation tost,
Our spring of action to ourselves is lost:
Tired, not determined, to the last we yield,
And what comes then is master of the field.
As the last image of that troubled heap,
When sense subsides, and fancy sports in sleep
(Though past the recollection of the thought),
Becomes the stuff of which our dream is wrought:
Something as dim to our internal view,
Is thus, perhaps, the cause of most we do.
   True, some are open, and to all men known;
Others so very close, they're hid from none
(So darkness strikes the sense no less than light),
Thus gracious Chandos is beloved at sight;
And every child hates Shylock, though his soul
Still sits at squat, and peeps not from its hole.

At half mankind when generous Manly raves,
All know 'tis virtue, for he thinks them knaves:
When universal homage Umbra pays,
All see 'tis vice, and itch of vulgar praise.
When flattery glares, all hate it in a queen,
While one there is who charms us with his spleen.

But these plain characters we rarely find;
Though strong the bent, yet quick the turns of mind:
Or puzzling contraries confound the whole;
Or affectations quite reverse the soul.
The dull, flat falsehood serves for policy;
And in the cunning, truth itself's a lie:
Unthought-of frailties cheat us in the wise;
The fool lies hid in inconsistencies.

See the same man, in vigour, in the gout;
Alone, in company; in place, or out;
Early at business, and at hazard late;
Mad at a fox-chase, wise at a debate;
Drunk at a borough, civil at a ball;
Friendly at Hackney, faithless at Whitehall.
Catius is ever moral, ever grave,
Thinks who endures a knave is next a knave,
Save just at dinner--then prefers, no doubt,
A rogue with venison to a saint without.

Who would not praise Patritio's high desert,
His hand unstained, his uncorrupted heart,
His comprehensive head! all interests weighed,
All Europe saved, yet Britain not betrayed.
He thanks you not, his pride is in piquet,
Newmarket-fame, and judgment at a bet.

What made (say Montagne, or more sage Charron)
Otho a warrior, Cromwell a buffoon?
A perjured prince a leaden saint revere,

A godless regent tremble at a star?
The throne a bigot keep, a genius quit,
Faithless through piety, and duped through wit?
Europe a woman, child, or dotard rule,
And just her wisest monarch made a fool?
  Know, God and Nature only are the same:
In man, the judgment shoots at flying game,
A bird of passage! gone as soon as found,
Now in the moon, perhaps, now under ground.
  In vain the sage, with retrospective eye,
Would from the apparent what conclude the why,
Infer the motive from the deed, and show,
That what we chanced was what we meant to do.
Behold! if fortune or a mistress frowns,
Some plunge in business, others shave their crowns:
To ease the soul of one oppressive weight,
This quits an empire, that embroils a state:
The same adust complexion has impelled
Charles to the convent, Philip to the field.
  Not always actions show the man: we find
Who does a kindness, is not therefore kind;
Perhaps prosperity becalmed his breast,
Perhaps the wind just shifted from the east:
Not therefore humble he who seeks retreat,
Pride guides his steps, and bids him shun the great:
Who combats bravely is not therefore brave,
He dreads a death-bed like the meanest slave:
Who reasons wisely is not therefore wise,
His pride in reasoning, not in acting lies.
  But grant that actions best discover man;
Take the most strong, and sort them as you can.
The few that glare each character must mark;
You balance not the many in the dark.

What will you do with such as disagree?
Suppress them, or miscall them policy?
Must then at once (the character to save)
The plain rough hero turn a crafty knave?
Alas! in truth the man but changed his mind,
Perhaps was sick, in love, or had not dined.
Ask why from Britain Caesar would retreat?
Caesar himself might whisper he was beat.
Why risk the world's great empire for a punk?
Caesar perhaps might answer he was drunk.
But, sage historians! 'tis your task to prove
One action conduct; one, heroic love.
   'Tis from high life high characters are drawn;
A saint in crape is twice a saint in lawn;
A judge is just, a chancellor juster still;
A gownman, learn'd; a bishop, what you will;
Wise, if a minister; but, if a king,
More wise, more learned, more just, more everything.
Court-virtues bear, like gems, the highest rate,
Born where Heaven's influence scarce can penetrate:
In life's low vale, the soil the virtues like,
They please as beauties, here as wonders strike.
Though the same sun with all-diffusive rays
Blush in the rose, and in the diamond blaze,
We prize the stronger effort of his power,
And justly set the gem above the flower.
   'Tis education forms the common mind;
Just as the twig is bent, the tree's inclined.
Boastful and rough, your first son is a squire;
The next a tradesman, meek, and much a liar;
Tom struts a soldier, open, bold, and brave;
Will sneaks a scrivener, an exceeding knave:
Is he a Churchman? then he's fond of power: }

A Quaker? sly: A Presbyterian? sour: }
A smart Freethinker? all things in an hour. }
  Ask men's opinions: Scoto now shall tell
How trade increases, and the world goes well;
Strike off his pension, by the setting sun,
And Britain, if not Europe, is undone.
  That gay Freethinker, a fine talker once,
What turns him now a stupid silent dunce?
Some god, or spirit he has lately found:
Or chanced to meet a minister that frowned.
Judge we by Nature? habit can efface,
Interest o'ercome, or policy take place:
By actions? those uncertainty divides:
By passions? these dissimulation hides:
Opinions? they still take a wider range:
Find, if you can, in what you cannot change.
  Manners with fortunes, humours turn with climes,
Tenets with books, and principles with times.

  Search then the ruling passion: there, alone,
The wild are constant, and the cunning known;
The fool consistent, and the false sincere;
Priests, princes, women, no dissemblers here.
This clue once found, unravels all the rest,
The prospect clears, and Wharton stands confest.
Wharton, the scorn and wonder of our days,
Whose ruling passion was the lust of praise:
Born with whate'er could win it from the wise,
Women and fools must like him or he dies;
Though wondering senates hung on all he spoke,
The club must hail him master of the joke.
Shall parts so various aim at nothing new!
He'll shine a Tully and a Wilmot too.

Then turns repentant, and his God adores
With the same spirit that he drinks and wh***s;
Enough if all around him but admire,
And now the punk applaud, and now the friar.
Thus with each gift of nature and of art,
And wanting nothing but an honest heart;
Grown all to all, from no one vice exempt;
And most contemptible, to shun contempt:
His passion still, to covet general praise,
His life, to forfeit it a thousand ways;
A constant bounty which no friend has made;
An angel tongue, which no man can persuade;
A fool, with more of wit than half mankind,
Too rash for thought, for action too refined:
A tyrant to the wife his heart approves;
A rebel to the very king he loves;
He dies, sad outcast of each church and state,
And, harder still! flagitious, yet not great.
Ask you why Wharton broke through every rule?
'Twas all for fear the knaves should call him fool.

   Nature well known, no prodigies remain,
Comets are regular, and Wharton plain.

   Yet, in this search, the wisest may mistake,
If second qualities for first they take.
When Catiline by rapine swelled his store;
When Caesar made a noble dame a wh***;
In this the lust, in that the avarice
Were means, not ends; ambition was the vice.
That very Caesar, born in Scipio's days,
Had aimed, like him, by chastity at praise.
Lucullus, when frugality could charm,
Had roasted turnips in the Sabine farm.

   In vain the observer eyes the builder's toil,

But quite mistakes the scaffold for the pile.
In this one passion man can strength enjoy,
As fits give vigour, just when they destroy.
Time, that on all things lays his lenient hand,
Yet tames not this; it sticks to our last sand.
Consistent in our follies and our sins,
Here honest Nature ends as she begins.

  Old politicians chew on wisdom past,
And totter on in business to the last;
As weak, as earnest, and as gravely out,
As sober Lanesb'row dancing in the gout.

  Behold a reverend sire, whom want of grace
Has made the father of a nameless race,
Shoved from the wall perhaps, or rudely pressed
By his own son, that passes by unblessed:
Still to his haunt he crawls on knocking knees,
And envies every sparrow that he sees.

  A salmon's belly, Helluo, was thy fate;
The doctor called, declares all help too late:
"Mercy!" cries Helluo, "mercy on my soul!
Is there no hope!--Alas!--then bring the jowl."

  The frugal crone, whom praying priests attend,
Still tries to save the hallowed taper's end,
Collects her breath, as ebbing life retires,
For one puff more, and in that puff expires.

  "Odious! in woollen! 'twould a saint provoke"
(Were the last words that poor Narcissa spoke);
"No, let a charming chintz, and Brussels lace
Wrap my cold limbs, and shade my lifeless face:
One would not, sure, be frightful when one's dead--
And--Betty--give this cheek a little red."

  The courtier smooth, who forty years had shined
An humble servant to all human kind,

Just brought out this, when scarce his tongue could stir,
"If--where I'm going--I could serve you, sir?"
"I give and I devise" (old Euclio said,
And sighed) "my lands and tenements to Ned."
"Your money, sir?" "My money, sir? what, all?
Why--if I must" (then wept)--"I give it Paul."
"The Manor, sir?"--"The Manor! hold," he cried,
"Not that,--I cannot part with that"--and died.
　And you! brave Cobham, to the latest breath
Shall feel your ruling passion strong in death:
Such in those moments as in all the past,
"Oh, save my country, Heaven!" shall be your last.

EPISTLE II. TO A LADY.

Of the Characters of Women.

Nothing so true as what you once let fall,
"Most women have no characters at all."
Matter too soft a lasting mark to bear,
And best distinguished by black, brown, or fair.
　How many pictures of one nymph we view,
All how unlike each other, all how true!
Arcadia's countess, here, in ermined pride,
Is, there, Pastora by a fountain side.
Here Fannia, leering on her own good man,
And there, a naked Leda with a swan.
Let then the fair one beautifully cry,
In Magdalen's loose hair, and lifted eye,
Or dressed in smiles of sweet Cecilia shine,
With simpering angels, palms, and harps divine;

Whether the charmer sinner it, or saint it,
If folly grow romantic, I must paint it.

Come then, the colours and the ground prepare!
Dip in the rainbow, trick her off in air;
Choose a firm cloud, before it fall, and in it
Catch, ere she change, the Cynthia of this minute.

Rufa, whose eye, quick-glancing o'er the park
Attracts each light gay meteor of a spark,
Agrees as ill with Rufa studying Locke,
As Sappho's diamonds with her dirty smock;
Or Sappho at her toilet's greasy task,
With Sappho fragrant at an evening masque:
So morning insects that in muck begun,
Shine, buzz, and fly-blow in the setting sun.

How soft is Silia! fearful to offend;
The frail one's advocate, the weak one's friend:
To her, Calista proved her conduct nice;
And good Simplicius asks of her advice.
Sudden, she storms! she raves! You tip the wink,
But spare your censure; Silia does not drink.
All eyes may see from what the change arose,
All eyes may see--a pimple on her nose.

Papillia, wedded to her am'rous spark,
Sighs for the shades--"How charming is a park!"
A park is purchased, but the fair he sees
All bathed in tears--"Oh, odious, odious trees!"

Ladies, like variegated tulips show;
'Tis to their changes half their charms we owe;

Fine by defect, and delicately weak,
Their happy spots the nice admirer take,
'Twas thus Calypso once each heart alarmed,
Awed without virtue, without beauty charmed;
Her tongue bewitched as oddly as her eyes,
Less wit than mimic, more a wit than wise;
Strange graces still, and stranger flights she had,
Was just not ugly, and was just not mad;
Yet ne'er so sure our passion to create,
As when she touched the brink of all we hate.

   Narcissa's nature, tolerably mild,
To make a wash, would hardly stew a child;
Has even been proved to grant a lover's prayer,
And paid a tradesman once to make him stare;
Gave alms at Easter, in a Christian trim,
And made a widow happy, for a whim.
Why then declare good-nature is her scorn,
When 'tis by that alone she can be borne?
Why pique all mortals, yet affect a name?
A fool to pleasure, yet a slave to fame:
Now deep in Taylor and the Book of Martyrs,
Now drinking citron with his grace and Chartres:
Now Conscience chills her, and now Passion burns;
And Atheism and Religion take their turns;
A very heathen in the carnal part,
Yet still a sad, good Christian at her heart.

   What then? let blood and body bear the fault,
Her head's untouched, that noble seat of thought:
Such this day's doctrine--in another fit
She sins with poets through pure love of wit.
What has not fired her bosom or her brain?

Caesar and Tall-boy, Charles and Charlemagne.
As Helluo, late dictator of the feast,
The nose of Hautgout, and the tip of taste,
Critic'd your wine, and analysed your meat,
Yet on plain pudding deigned at home to eat;
So Philomede, lecturing all mankind
On the soft passion, and the taste refined,
The address, the delicacy--stoops at once,
And makes her hearty meal upon a dunce.
    Flavia's a wit, has too much sense to pray;
To toast our wants and wishes, is her way;
Nor asks of God, but of her stars, to give
The mighty blessing, "while we live, to live."
Then all for death, that opiate of the soul!
Lucretia's dagger, Rosamonda's bowl.
Say, what can cause such impotence of mind?
A spark too fickle, or a spouse too kind.
Wise wretch! with pleasures too refined to please;
With too much spirit to be e'er at ease;
With too much quickness ever to be taught;
With too much thinking to have common thought:
You purchase pain with all that joy can give,
And die of nothing but a rage to live.
    Turn then from wits; and look on Simo's mate,
No ass so meek, no ass so obstinate.
Or her, that owns her faults, but never mends,
Because she's honest, and the best of friends.
Or her, whose life the Church and scandal share,
For ever in a passion, or a prayer.
Or her, who laughs at hell, but (like her Grace)
Cries, "Ah! how charming, if there's no such place!"
Or who in sweet vicissitude appears
Of mirth and opium, ratafie and tears,

The daily anodyne, and nightly draught,
To kill those foes to fair ones, time and thought.
Woman and fool are two hard things to hit;
For true no-meaning puzzles more than wit.
  But what are these to great Atossa's mind?
Scarce once herself, by turns all womankind!
Who, with herself, or others, from her birth
Finds all her life one warfare upon earth:
Shines in exposing knaves, and painting fools,
Yet is, whate'er she hates and ridicules.
No thought advances, but her eddy brain
Whisks it about, and down it goes again.
Full sixty years the world has been her trade,
The wisest fool much time has ever made
From loveless youth to unrespected age,
No passion gratified except her rage.
So much the fury still outran the wit,
The pleasure missed her, and the scandal hit.
Who breaks with her, provokes revenge from hell,
But he's a bolder man who dares be well.
Her every turn with violence pursued,
Nor more a storm her hate than gratitude:
To that each passion turns, or soon or late;
Love, if it makes her yield, must make her hate:
Superiors? death! and equals? what a curse!
But an inferior not dependent? worse.
Offend her, and she knows not to forgive;
Oblige her, and she'll hate you while you live:
But die, and she'll adore you--then the bust
And temple rise--then fall again to dust.
Last night, her lord was all that's good and great;
A knave this morning, and his will a cheat.
Strange! by the means defeated of the ends,

By spirit robbed of power, by warmth of friend
By wealth of followers! without one distress
Sick of herself through very selfishness!
Atossa, cursed with every granted prayer,
Childless with all her children, wants an heir.
To heirs unknown descends the unguarded store,
Or wanders, Heaven-directed, to the poor.
　Pictures like these, dear madam, to design,
Asks no firm hand, and no unerring line;
Some wandering touches, some reflected light,
Some flying stroke alone can hit 'em right:
For how should equal colours do the knack?
Chameleons who can paint in white and black?
　"Yet Chloe sure was formed without a spot"--
Nature in her then erred not, but forgot.
"With every pleasing, every prudent part,
Say, what can Chloe want?"--She wants a heart.
She speaks, behaves, and acts just as she ought;
But never, never, reached one generous thought.
Virtue she finds too painful an endeavour,
Content to dwell in decencies for ever.
So very reasonable, so unmoved,
As never yet to love, or to be loved.
She, while her lover pants upon her breast,
Can mark the figures on an Indian chest;
And when she sees her friend in deep despair,
Observes how much a chintz exceeds mohair.
Forbid it, Heaven, a favour or a debt
She e'er should cancel--but she may forget.
Safe is your secret still in Chloe's ear;
But none of Chloe's shall you ever hear.
Of all her dears she never slandered one,
But cares not if a thousand are undone.

Would Chloe know if you're alive or dead?
She bids her footman put it in her head.
Chloe is prudent--would you too be wise?
Then never break your heart when Chloe dies.
  One certain portrait may (I grant) be seen,
Which Heaven has varnished out, and made a **Queen**.
The same for ever! and described by all
With truth and goodness, as with crown and ball.
Poets heap virtues, painters gems at will,
And show their zeal, and hide their want of skill.
'Tis well--but, artists! who can paint or write,
To draw the naked is your true delight.
That robe of quality so struts and swells,
None see what parts of nature it conceals:
The exactest traits of body or of mind,
We owe to models of an humble kind.
If Queensbury to strip there's no compelling,
'Tis from a handmaid we must take a Helen,
From peer or bishop 'tis no easy thing
To draw the man who loves his God or king:
Alas! I copy (or my draught would fail)
From honest Mah'met, or plain Parson Hale.
  But grant in public men sometimes are shown,
A woman's seen in private life alone:
Our bolder talents in full light displayed;
Your virtues open fairest in the shade.
Bred to disguise, in public 'tis you hide;
There, none distinguish 'twixt your shame or pride,
Weakness or delicacy; all so nice,
That each may seem a virtue or a vice.
  In men, we various ruling passions find;
In women, two almost divide the kind:
Those, only fixed they first or last obey--

The love of pleasure, and the love of sway.
   That, Nature gives; and where the lesson taught
Is but to please, can pleasure seem a fault?
Experience, this; by man's oppression curst,
They seek the second not to lose the first.
   Men, some to business, some to pleasure take;
But every woman is at heart a rake:
Men, some to quiet, some to public strife;
But every lady would be queen for life.
   Yet mark the fate of a whole sex of queens!
Power all their end, but beauty all the means:
In youth they conquer, with so wild a rage,
As leaves them scarce a subject in their age:
For foreign glory, foreign joy, they roam;
No thought of peace or happiness at home.
But wisdom's triumph is well-timed retreat,
As hard a science to the fair as great!
Beauties, like tyrants, old and friendless grown,
Yet hate repose, and dread to be alone,
Worn out in public, weary every eye,
Nor leave one sigh behind them when they die.
   Pleasures the sex, as children birds, pursue,
Still out of reach, yet never out of view;
Sure, if they catch, to spoil the toy at most,
To covet flying, and regret when lost:
At last, to follies youth could scarce defend,
It grows their age's prudence to pretend;
Ashamed to own they gave delight before,
Reduced to feign it, when they give no more:
As hags hold Sabbaths, less for joy than spite,
So these their merry, miserable night;
Still round and round the ghosts of beauty glide,
And haunt the places where their honour died.

See how the world its veterans rewards!
A youth of frolics, an old age of cards;
Fair to no purpose, artful to no end;
Young without lovers, old without a friend;
A fop their passion, but their prize a sot;
Alive, ridiculous; and dead, forgot!

Ah! friend! to dazzle let the vain design;
To raise the thought and touch the heart be thine!
That charm shall grow, while what fatigues the ring,
Flaunts and goes down, an unregarded thing:
So when the sun's broad beam has tired the sight,
All mild ascends the moon's more sober light;
Serene in virgin modesty she shines,
And unobserved the glaring orb declines.

Oh! blest with temper whose unclouded ray
Can make to-morrow cheerful as to-day,
She, who can love a sister's charms, or hear
Sighs for a daughter with unwounded ear;
She, who ne'er answers till a husband cools,
Or, if she rules him, never shows she rules;
Charms by accepting, by submitting sways,
Yet has her humour most, when she obeys;
Let fops or fortune fly which way they will;
Disdains all loss of tickets, or Codille:
Spleen, vapours, or small-pox, above them all,
And mistress of herself, though China fall.

And yet, believe me, good as well as ill,
Woman's at best a contradiction still.
Heaven, when it strives to polish all it can
Its last best work, but forms a softer man;
Picks from each sex, to make the fav'rite blest,
Your love of pleasure, or desire of rest:
Blends, in exception to all general rules,

Your taste of follies, with our scorn of fools:
Reserve with frankness, art with truth allied,
Courage with softness, modesty with pride;
Fixed principles, with fancy ever new;
Shakes all together, and produces--You.
   Be this a woman's fame: with this unblest,
Toasts live a scorn, and queens may die a jest.
This Phoebus promised (I forget the year)
When those blue eyes first opened on the sphere;
Ascendant Phoebus watched that hour with care,
Averted half your parents' simple prayer,
And gave you beauty, but denied the pelf
That buys your sex a tyrant o'er itself.
The gen'rous god, who wit and gold refines,
And ripens spirits as he ripens mines,
Kept dross for duchesses--the world shall know it--
To you gave sense, good-humour, and a poet.

EPISTLE III. TO ALLEN LORD BATHURST.

ARGUMENT.

Of the use of Riches.

That it is known to few, most falling into one of the extremes, Avarice
or Profusion, v.1, etc. The point discussed, whether the invention of
money has been more commodious or pernicious to Mankind, v.21 to 77.
That
Riches, either to the Avaricious or the Prodigal, cannot afford
Happiness, scarcely Necessaries, v.89-160. That Avarice is an absolute
Frenzy, without an end or purpose, v.113, etc., 152. Conjectures about

the motives of Avaricious men, v.121 to 153. That the conduct of men, with respect to Riches, can only be accounted for by the Order of Providence, which works the general good out of extremes, and brings all to its great End by perpetual Revolutions, v.161 to 178. How a Miser acts upon Principles which appear to him reasonable, v.179. How a Prodigal does the same, v.199. The due Medium and true use of Riches, v.219. The Man of Ross, v.250. The fate of the Profuse and the Covetous, in two examples; both miserable in Life and in Death, v.300, etc. The Story of Sir Balaam, v.339 to the end.

   P. Who shall decide, when doctors disagree,
And soundest casuists doubt, like you and me?
You hold the word, from Jove to Momus given,
That man was made the standing jest of Heaven;
And gold but sent to keep the fools in play,
For some to heap, and some to throw away.
   But I, who think more highly of our kind,
(And surely, Heaven and I are of a mind)
Opine, that Nature, as in duty bound,
Deep hid the shining mischief under ground:
But when by man's audacious labour won,
Flamed forth this rival to its sire, the sun,
Then careful Heaven supplied two sorts of men,
To squander these, and those to hide again.
   Like doctors thus, when much dispute has past,
We find our tenets just the same at last.
Both fairly owning Riches, in effect,
No grace of Heaven or token of th' elect;
Given to the fool, the mad, the vain, the evil,
To Ward, to Waters, Chartres, and the devil.
   B. What Nature wants, commodious gold bestows,
'Tis thus we eat the bread another sows.
   P. But how unequal it bestows, observe;

'Tis thus we riot, while, who sow it, starve:
What Nature wants (a phrase I much distrust)
Extends to luxury, extends to lust:
Useful, I grant, it serves what life requires,
But, dreadful too, the dark assassin hires.
   B. Trade it may help, society extend.
   P. But lures the pirate, and corrupts the friend.
   B. It raises armies in a nation's aid.
   P. But bribes a senate, and the land's betrayed.
In vain may heroes fight, and patriots rave;
If secret gold sap on from knave to knave.
Once, we confess, beneath the patriot's cloak,
From the cracked bag the dropping guinea spoke,
And jingling down the back-stairs, told the crew,
"Old Cato is as great a rogue as you."
Blest paper-credit! last and best supply!
That lends corruption lighter wings to fly!
Gold imped by thee can compass hardest things,
Can pocket states, can fetch or carry kings;
A single leaf shall waft an army o'er,
Or ship off senates to a distant shore;
A leaf, like Sibyl's, scatter to and fro
Our fates and fortunes, as the winds shall blow:
Pregnant with thousands flits the scrap unseen,
And silent sells a king, or buys a queen.
  Oh! that such bulky bribes as all might see,
Still, as of old, encumbered villainy!
Could France or Rome divert our brave designs,
With all their brandies or with all their wines?
What could they more than knights and squires confound,
Or water all the Quorum ten miles round?
A statesman's slumbers how this speech would spoil!
"Sir, Spain has sent a thousand jars of oil;

Huge bales of British cloth blockade the door;
A hundred oxen at your levee roar."
  Poor Avarice one torment more would find;
Nor could Profusion squander all in kind.
Astride his cheese Sir Morgan might we meet;
And Worldly crying coals from street to street,
Whom with a wig so wild, and mien so mazed,
Pity mistakes for some poor tradesman crazed.
Had Colepepper's whole wealth been hops and hogs,
Could he himself have sent it to the dogs?
His Grace will game: to White's a bull be led,
With spurning heels and with a butting head.
To White's be carried, as to ancient games,
Fair coursers, vases, and alluring dames.
Shall then Uxorio, if the stakes he sweep,
Bear home six w****s, and make his lady weep?
Or soft Adonis, so perfumed and fine,
Drive to St. James's a whole herd of swine?
Oh, filthy cheek on all industrious skill,
To spoil the nation's last great trade, Quadrille!
Since then, my lord, on such a world we fall,
What say you? B. Say? Why, take it, gold and all.
  P. What Riches give us let us then inquire:
Meat, fire, and clothes. B. What more? P. Meat, clothes, and fire.
Is this too little? would you more than live?
Alas! 'tis more than Turner finds they give.
Alas! 'tis more than (all his visions past)
Unhappy Wharton, waking, found at last!
What can they give? to dying Hopkins, heirs;
To Chartres, vigour; Japhet, nose and ears?
Can they in gems bid pallid Hippia glow,
In Fulvia's buckle ease the throbs below;
Or heal, old Narses, thy obscener ail,

With all th' embroid'ry plastered at thy tail?
They might (were Harpax not too wise to spend)
Give Harpax' self the blessing of a friend;
Or find some doctor that would save the life
Of wretched Shylock, spite of Shylock's wife:
But thousands die, without or this or that,
Die, and endow a college, or a cat.
To some, indeed, Heaven grants the happier fate,
T' enrich a bastard, or a son they hate.

  Perhaps you think the poor might have their part?
Bond damns the poor, and hates them from his heart:
The grave Sir Gilbert holds it for a rule,
That "every man in want is knave or fool:"
"God cannot love," says Blunt, with tearless eyes,
"The wretch He starves"--and piously denies:
But the good bishop, with a meeker air,
Admits, and leaves them--Providence's care.

  Yet, to be just to these poor men of pelf,
Each does but hate his neighbour as himself:
Damned to the mines, an equal fate betides
The slave that digs it, and the slave that hides.

  B. Who suffer thus, mere charity should own,
Must act on motives powerful, though unknown.

  P. Some war, some plague, or famine they foresee,
Some revelation hid from you and me.
Why Shylock wants a meal, the cause is found--
He thinks a loaf will rise to fifty pound.
What made directors cheat in South-Sea year?
To live on venison when it sold so dear.
Ask you why Phryne the whole auction buys?
Phryne foresees a general excise.
Why she and Sappho raise that monstrous sum?
Alas! they fear a man will cost a plum.

Wise Peter sees the world's respect for gold,
And therefore hopes this nation may be sold:
Glorious ambition! Peter, swell thy store,
And be what Rome's great Didius was before.

The crown of Poland, venal twice an age,
To just three millions stinted modest Gage.
But nobler scenes Maria's dreams unfold,
Hereditary realms, and worlds of gold.
Congenial souls! whose life one av'rice joins,
And one fate buries in th' Asturian mines.

Much injured Blunt! why bears he Britain's hate?
A wizard told him in these words our fate:
"At length corruption, like a gen'ral flood
(So long by watchful Ministers withstood),
Shall deluge all; and av'rice, creeping on,
Spread like a low-born mist, and blot the sun;
Statesman and patriot ply alike the stocks,
Peeress and butler share alike the box,
And judges job, and bishops bite the town,
And mighty dukes pack cards for half-a-crown.
See Britain sunk in Lucre's sordid charms,
And France revenged of Anne's and Edward's arms!"
'Twas no Court-badge, great Scriv'ner! fired thy brain,
Nor lordly luxury, nor City gain:
No, 'twas thy righteous end, ashamed to see
Senates degen'rate, patriots disagree,
And, nobly wishing party-rage to cease,
To buy both sides, and give thy country peace.

"All this is madness," cries a sober sage:
But who, my friend, has reason in his rage?
"The ruling passion, be it what it will,
The ruling passion conquers reason still."
Less mad the wildest whimsey we can frame,

Than even that passion, if it has no aim;
For though such motives folly you may call,
The folly's greater to have none at all.
  Hear then the truth: "'Tis Heaven each passion sends,
And different men directs to different ends.
Extremes in nature equal good produce,
Extremes in man concur to gen'ral use."
Ask we what makes one keep, and one bestow?
That POWER who bids the ocean ebb and flow,
Bids seed-time, harvest, equal course maintain,
Through reconciled extremes of drought and rain,
Builds life on death, on change duration founds,
And gives th' eternal wheels to know their rounds.
  Riches, like insects, when concealed they lie,
Wait but for wings, and in their season fly.
Who sees pale Mammon pine amidst his store,
Sees but a backward steward for the poor;
This year a reservoir, to keep and spare;
The next, a fountain, spouting through his heir,
In lavish streams to quench a country's thirst,
And men and dogs shall drink him till they burst.
  Old Cotta shamed his fortune and his birth,
Yet was not Cotta void of wit or worth:
What though (the use of barbarous spits forgot)
His kitchen vied in coolness with his grot?
His court with nettles, moats with cresses stored,
With soups unbought and salads blessed his board?
If Cotta lived on pulse, it was no more
Than Brahmins, saints, and sages did before;
To cram the rich was prodigal expense,
And who would take the poor from Providence?
Like some lone Chartreux stands the good old hall,
Silence without, and fasts within the wall;

No raftered roofs with dance and tabor sound,
No noontide bell invites the country round;
Tenants with sighs the smokeless towers survey,
And turn th' unwilling steeds another way;
Benighted wanderers, the forest o'er,
Curse the saved candle and unopening door;
While the gaunt mastiff growling at the gate,
Affrights the beggar whom he longs to eat.
  Not so his son; he marked this oversight,
And then mistook reverse of wrong for right.
(For what to shun will no great knowledge need;
But what to follow is a task indeed.)
Yet sure, of qualities deserving praise,
More go to ruin fortunes, than to raise.
What slaughtered hecatombs, what floods of wine,
Fill the capacious squire, and deep divine!
Yet no mean motive this profusion draws;
His oxen perish in his country's cause;
'Tis George and Liberty that crowns the cup,
And zeal for that great house which eats him up.
The woods recede around the naked seat;
The sylvans groan--no matter--for the fleet;
Next goes his wool--to clothe our valiant bands;
Last, for his country's love, he sells his lands.
To town he comes, completes the nation's hope,
And heads the bold train-bands, and burns a Pope.
And shall not Britain now reward his toils,
Britain, that pays her patriots with her spoils?
In vain at Court the bankrupt pleads his cause,
His thankless country leaves him to her laws.
  The sense to value riches, with the art
T' enjoy them, and the virtue to impart,
Not meanly, nor ambitiously pursued,

Not sunk by sloth, nor raised by servitude;
To balance fortune by a just expense,
Join with economy, magnificence;
With splendour, charity; with plenty, health;
O teach us, Bathurst! yet unspoiled by wealth!
That secret rare, between the extremes to move
Of mad good-nature, and of mean self-love.
   B. To worth or want well weighed, be bounty given,
And ease, or emulate, the care of Heaven
(Whose measure full o'erflows on human race);
Mend Fortune's fault, and justify her grace.
Wealth in the gross is death, but life diffused;
As poison heals, in just proportion used:
In heaps, like ambergrise, a stink it lies,
But well dispersed, is incense to the skies.
   P. Who starves by nobles, or with nobles eats?
The wretch that trusts them, and the rogue that cheats.
Is there a lord who knows a cheerful noon
Without a fiddler, flatterer, or buffoon?
Whose table, wit or modest merit share,
Unelbowed by a gamester, pimp, or play'r?
Who copies yours or Oxford's better part,
To ease the oppressed, and raise the sinking heart?
Where'er he shines, O Fortune, gild the scene,
And angels guard him in the golden mean!
There, English bounty yet awhile may stand,
And Honour linger ere it leaves the land.
   But all our praises why should lords engross?
Rise, honest Muse! and sing the Man of Ross:
Pleased Vaga echoes through her winding bounds,
And rapid Severn hoarse applause resounds.
Who hung with woods you mountain's sultry brow?
From the dry rock who bade the waters flow?

Not to the skies in useless columns tost,
Or in proud falls magnificently lost,
But clear and artless, pouring through the plain
Health to the sick, and solace to the swain.
Whose causeway parts the vale with shady rows?
Whose seats the weary traveller repose?
Who taught that heaven-directed spire to rise?
"The Man of Ross," each lisping babe replies.
Behold the market-place with poor o'erspread!
The Man of Ross divides the weekly bread;
He feeds yon almshouse, neat, but void of state,
Where age and want sit smiling at the gate;
Him portioned maids, apprenticed orphans blest,
The young who labour, and the old who rest.
Is any sick? the Man of Ross relieves,
Prescribes, attends, the medicine makes, and gives.
Is there a variance? enter but his door,
Baulked are the courts, and contest is no more.
Despairing quacks with curses fled the place,
And vile attorneys, now a useless race.
   B. Thrice happy man! enabled to pursue
What all so wish, but want the power to do!
Oh say, what sums that generous hand supply?
What mines, to swell that boundless charity?
   P. Of debts, and taxes, wife and children clear,
This man possest--five hundred pounds a year.
Blush, grandeur, blush! proud courts, withdraw your blaze!
Ye little stars, hide your diminished rays!
   B. And what? no monument, inscription, stone?
His race, his form, his name almost unknown?
   P. Who builds a church to God, and not to Fame,
Will never mark the marble with his name;
Go, search it there, where to be born and die,

Of rich and poor makes all the history;
Enough, that virtue filled the space between;
Proved, by the ends of being, to have been.
When Hopkins dies, a thousand lights attend
The wretch, who living saved a candle's end:
Shouldering God's altar a vile image stands,
Belies his features, nay, extends his hands;
That livelong wig, which Gorgon's self might own,
Eternal buckle takes in Parian stone.
Behold what blessings wealth to life can lend!
And see what comfort it affords our end.
    In the worst inn's worst room, with mat half-hung,
The floors of plaster, and the walls of dung,
On once a flock-bed, but repaired with straw,
With tape-tied curtains, never meant to draw,
The George and Garter dangling from that bed
Where tawdry yellow strove with dirty red,
Great Villiers lies--alas! how changed from him,
That life of pleasure, and that soul of whim!--
Gallant and gay, in Cliveden's proud alcove,
The bower of wanton Shrewsbury and love;
Or just as gay, at council, in a ring
Of mimic'd statesmen and their merry king.
No wit to flatter left of all his store!
No fool to laugh at, which he valued more.
There, victor of his health, of fortune, friends,
And fame, this lord of useless thousands ends.
    His grace's fate sage Cutler could foresee,
And well (he thought) advised him, "Live like me."
As well his grace replied, "Like you, Sir John?
That I can do, when all I have is gone."
Resolve me, Reason, which of these is worse,
Want with a full, or with an empty purse?

Thy life more wretched, Cutler, was confessed,
Arise, and tell me, was thy death more blessed?
Cutler saw tenants break, and houses fall,
For very want; he could not build a wall.
His only daughter in a stranger's power,
For very want; he could not pay a dower.
A few grey hairs his reverend temples crowned,
'Twas very want that sold them for two pound.
What even denied a cordial at his end,
Banished the doctor, and expelled the friend?
What but a want, which you perhaps think mad,
Yet numbers feel the want of what he had!
Cutler and Brutus, dying, both exclaim,
"Virtue! and wealth! what are ye but a name!"
   Say, for such worth are other worlds prepared?
Or are they both in this their own reward?
A knotty point! to which we now proceed.
But you are tired--I'll tell a tale. B. Agreed.
    P. Where London's column, pointing at the skies,
Like a tall bully, lifts the head, and lies;
There dwelt a citizen of sober fame,
A plain good man, and Balaam was his name;
Religious, punctual, frugal, and so forth;
His word would pass for more than he was worth.
One solid dish his week-day meal affords,
An added pudding solemnised the Lord's;
Constant at church, and Change; his gains were sure,
His givings rare, save farthings to the poor.
The devil was piqued such saintship to behold,
And longed to tempt him like good Job of old:
But Satan now is wiser than of yore,
And tempts by making rich, not making poor.
   Roused by the prince of Air, the whirlwinds sweep

The surge, and plunge his father in the deep;
Then full against his Cornish lands they roar,
And two rich shipwrecks bless the lucky shore.
    Sir Balaam now, he lives like other folks,
He takes his chirping pint, and cracks his jokes;
"Live like yourself," was soon my lady's word;
And lo! two puddings smoked upon the board.
    Asleep and naked as an Indian lay,
An honest factor stole a gem away:
He pledged it to the knight; the knight had wit,
So kept the diamond, and the rogue was bit.
Some scruple rose, but thus he eased his thought,
"I'll now give sixpence where I gave a groat;
Where once I went to church, I'll now go twice--
And am so clear, too, of all other vice."
    The Tempter saw his time; the work he plied;
Stocks and subscriptions pour on every side,
'Till all the demon makes his full descent
In one abundant shower of cent. per cent.,
Sinks deep within him, and possesses whole,
Then dubs director, and secures his soul.
    Behold Sir Balaam, now a man of spirit,
Ascribes his gettings to his parts and merit;
What late he called a blessing, now was wit,
And God's good Providence, a lucky hit.
Things change their titles, as our manners turn;
His counting-house employed the Sunday morn;
Seldom at church ('twas such a busy life),
But duly sent his family and wife.
There (so the devil ordained) one Christmas tide
My good old lady catched a cold and died.
    A nymph of quality admires our knight;
He marries, bows at court, and grows polite:

Leaves the dull cits, and joins (to please the fair)
The well bred c*ck**ds in St. James's air;
First, for his son a gay commission buys,
Who drinks and fights, and in a duel dies;
His daughter flaunts a viscount's tawdry wife;
She bears a coronet and ---- for life.
In Britain's senate he a seat obtains,
And one more pensioner St. Stephen gains.
My lady falls to play; so bad her chance,
He must repair it; takes a bribe from France;
The House impeach him; Coningsby harangues;
The Court forsake him, and Sir Balaam hangs;
Wife, son, and daughter, Satan! are thine own,
His wealth, yet dearer, forfeit to the Crown:
The Devil and the King divide the prize,
And sad Sir Balaam curses God and dies.

EPISTLE IV. TO RICHARD BOYLE, EARL OF BURLINGTON.

ARGUMENT.

Of the Use of Riches.

The Vanity of Expense in people of Wealth and Quality. The abuse of the
word Taste, v.13. That the first Principle and foundation, in this as in
everything else, is Good Sense, v.40. The chief Proof of it is to
follow Nature even in works of mere Luxury and Elegance. Instanced in
Architecture and Gardening, where all must be adapted to the Genius and
Use of the Place, and the Beauties not forced into it, but resulting from

it, v.**50**. How men are disappointed in their most expensive undertakings, for want of this true Foundation, without which nothing can please long, if at all: and the best Examples and Rules will but be perverted into something burdensome or ridiculous, v.65, etc., to 92. A description of the false Taste of Magnificence; the first grand Error of which is to imagine that Greatness consists in the size and dimension, instead of the Proportion and Harmony of the whole, v.97, and the second, either in joining together Parts incoherent, or too minutely resembling, or in the Repetition of the same too frequently, v.105, etc. A word or two of false Taste in Books, in Music, in Painting, even in Preaching and Prayer, and lastly in Entertainments, v.133, etc. Yet Providence is justified in giving Wealth to be squandered in this manner, since it is dispersed to the poor and laborious part of mankind, v.169 (recurring to what is laid down in the first book, Ep. ii., and in the Epistle preceding this, v.159, etc.). What are the proper objects of Magnificence, and a proper field for the Expense of Great Men, v.177, etc., and finally, the Great and Public Works which become a Prince, v.191 to the end.

'Tis strange, the miser should his cares employ
To gain those riches he can ne'er enjoy:
Is it less strange, the prodigal should waste
His wealth, to purchase what he ne'er can taste?
Not for himself he sees, or hears, or eats;
Artists must choose his pictures, music, meats:
He buys for Topham, drawings and designs,
For Pembroke, statues, dirty gods, and coins;
Rare monkish manuscripts for Hearne alone,
And books for Mead, and butterflies for Sloane.
Think we all these are for himself? no more
Than his fine wife, alas! or finer w***e.
  For what has Virro painted, built, and planted?
Only to show, how many tastes he wanted.

What brought Sir Visto's ill-got wealth to waste?
Some demon whispered, "Visto! have a taste."
Heaven visits with a taste the wealthy fool,
And needs no rod but Ripley with a rule.
See! sportive Fate, to punish awkward pride,
Bids Bubo build, and sends him such a guide.
A standing sermon, at each year's expense,
That never coxcomb reached magnificence!
   You show us, Rome was glorious, not profuse,
And pompous buildings once were things of use.
Yet shall, my lord, your just, your noble rules
Fill half the land with imitating fools;
Who random drawings from your sheets shall take,
And of one beauty many blunders make;
Load some vain church with old theatric state,
Turn arcs of triumph to a garden-gate;
Reverse your ornaments, and hang them all
On some patched dog-hole eked with ends of wall;
Then clap four slices of pilaster on 't,
That, laced with bits of rustic, makes a front
Shall call the winds through long arcades to roar,
Proud to catch cold at a Venetian door;
Conscious they act a true Palladian part,
And, if they starve, they starve by rules of art.
   Oft have you hinted to your brother peer
A certain truth, which many buy too dear:
Something there is more needful than expense,
And something previous even to taste--'tis sense.
Good sense, which only is the gift of Heaven,
And though no science, fairly worth the seven:
A light, which in yourself you must perceive:
Jones and Le Notre have it not to give.
   To build, to plant, whatever you intend,

To rear the column, or the arch to bend,
To swell the terrace, or to sink the grot;
In all, let Nature never be forgot.
But treat the goddess like a modest fair,
Nor over-dress, nor leave her wholly bare;
Let not each beauty everywhere be spied,
Where half the skill is decently to hide.
He gains all points, who pleasingly confounds,
Surprises, varies, and conceals the bounds.
    Consult the genius of the place in all;
That tells the waters or to rise or fall,
Or helps the ambitious hill the heavens to scale,
Or scoops in circling theatres the vale;
Calls in the country, catches opening glades,
Joins willing woods, and varies shades from shades;
Now breaks, or now directs, the intending lines;
Paints as you plant, and, as you work, designs.
    Still follow sense, of every art the soul,
Parts answering parts shall slide into a whole,
Spontaneous beauties all around advance,
Start even from difficulty, strike from chance;
Nature shall join you; Time shall make it grow
A work to wonder at--perhaps a Stowe.
    Without it, proud Versailles, thy glory falls;
And Nero's terraces desert their walls:
The vast parterres a thousand hands shall make;
Lo! Cobham comes, and floats them with a lake:
Or cut wide views through mountains to the plain,
You'll wish your hill or sheltered seat again.
Even in an ornament its place remark,
Nor in a hermitage set Dr. Clarke.
    Behold Villario's ten years' toil complete:
His quincunx darkens, his espaliers meet;

The wood supports the plain, the parts unite,
And strength of shade contends with strength of light;
A waving glow the bloomy beds display,
Blushing in bright diversities of day,
With silver-quivering rills meandered o'er--
Enjoy them, you! Villario can no more;
Tired of the scene parterres and fountains yield,
He finds at last he better likes a field.

   Through his young woods how pleased Sabinus strayed,
Or sat delighted in the thickening shade,
With annual joy the reddening shoots to greet,
Or see the stretching branches long to meet!
His son's fine taste an opener vista loves,
Foe to the Dryads of his father's groves;
One boundless green, or flourished carpet views,
With all the mournful family of yews;
The thriving plants, ignoble broomsticks made,
Now sweep those alleys they were born to shade.

   At Timon's villa let us pass a day,
Where all cry out, "What sums are thrown away!"
So proud, so grand; of that stupendous air,
Soft and agreeable come never there.
Greatness, with Timon, dwells in such a draught
As brings all Brobdingnag before your thought.
To compass this, his building is a town,
His pond an ocean, his parterre a down:
Who but must laugh, the master when he sees,
A puny insect, shivering at a breeze!
Lo, what huge heaps of littleness around!
The whole, a laboured quarry above ground;
Two Cupids squirt before; a lake behind
Improves the keenness of the northern wind.
His gardens next your admiration call,

On every side you look, behold the wall!
No pleasing intricacies intervene,
No artful wildness to perplex the scene;
Grove nods at grove, each alley has a brother,
And half the platform just reflects the other.
The suffering eye inverted Nature sees,
Trees cut to statues, statues thick as trees
With here a fountain, never to be played;
And there a summer-house, that knows no shade;
Here Amphitrite sails through myrtle bowers;
There gladiators fight or die in flowers;
Unwatered see the drooping sea-horse mourn,
And swallows roost in Nilus' dusty urn.
   My lord advances with majestic mien,
Smit with the mighty pleasure to be seen:
But soft--by regular approach--not yet--
First through the length of yon hot terrace sweat;
And when up ten steep slopes you've dragged your thighs,
Just at his study door he'll bless your eyes.
   His study! with what authors is it stored?
In books, not authors, curious is my lord;
To all their dated backs he turns you round:
These Aldus printed, those Du Sueil has bound,
Lo, some are vellum, and the rest as good
For all his lordship knows, but they are wood.
For Locke or Milton 'tis in vain to look;
These shelves admit not any modern book.
   And now the chapel's silver bell you hear,
That summons you to all the pride of prayer;
Light quirks of music, broken and uneven,
Make the soul dance upon a jig to heaven.
On painted ceilings you devoutly stare,
Where sprawl the saints of Verrio or Laguerre,

On gilded clouds in fair expansion lie,
And bring all Paradise before your eye.
To rest, the cushion and soft Dean invite,
Who never mentions hell to ears polite.
  But hark! the chiming clocks to dinner call;
A hundred footsteps scrape the marble hall:
The rich buffet well-coloured serpents grace,
And gaping Tritons spew to wash your face.
Is this a dinner? this a genial room?
No, 'tis a temple, and a hecatomb.
A solemn sacrifice, performed in state,
You drink by measure, and to minutes eat.
So quick retires each flying course, you'd swear
Sancho's dread doctor and his wand were there.
Between each act the trembling salvers ring,
From soup to sweet-wine, and God bless the King.
In plenty starving, tantalised in state,
And complaisantly helped to all I hate,
Treated, caressed, and tired, I take my leave,
Sick of his civil pride from morn to eve;
I curse such lavish cost and little skill,
And swear no day was ever past so ill.
  Yet hence the poor are clothed, the hungry fed;
Health to himself, and to his infants bread
The labourer bears; what his hard heart denies
His charitable vanity supplies.
  Another age shall see the golden ear
Embrown the slope, and nod on the parterre,
Deep harvests bury all his pride has planned,
And laughing Ceres re-assume the land.
  Who then shall grace, or who improve the soil?
Who plants like Bathurst, or who builds like Boyle.
'Tis use alone that sanctifies expense,

And splendour borrows all her rays from sense.
   His father's acres who enjoys in peace,
Or makes his neighbours glad, if he increase:
Whose cheerful tenants bless their yearly toil,
Yet to their lord owe more than to the soil;
Whose ample lawns are not ashamed to feed
The milky heifer and deserving steed;
Whose rising forests, not for pride or show,
But future buildings, future navies, grow:
Let his plantations stretch from down to down,
First shade a country, and then raise a town.
   You too proceed! make falling arts your care,
Erect new wonders, and the old repair;
Jones and Palladio to themselves restore,
And be whate'er Vitruvius was before:
'Till kings call forth the ideas of your mind
(Proud to accomplish what such hands denied)
Bid harbours open, public ways extend,
Bid temples, worthier of the god, ascend;
Bid the broad arch the dangerous flood contain,
The mole projected break the roaring main;
Back to his bounds their subject sea command,
And roll obedient rivers through the land:
These honours peace to happy Britain brings,
These are imperial works, and worthy kings.

EPISTLE V. TO MR. ADDISON.

Occasioned by his Dialogues on Medals.

See the wild waste of all-devouring years!

How Rome her own sad sepulchre appears,
With nodding arches, broken temples spread!
The very tombs now vanished like their dead!
Imperial wonders raised on nations spoiled,
Where mixed with slaves the groaning martyr toiled:
Huge theatres, that now unpeopled woods,
Now drained a distant country of her floods:
Fanes, which admiring gods with pride survey,
Statues of men, scarce less alive than they!
Some felt the silent stroke of mouldering age,
Some hostile fury, some religious rage.
Barbarian blindness, Christian zeal conspire,
And Papal piety, and Gothic fire.
Perhaps, by its own ruins saved from flame,
Some buried marble half preserves a name;
That name the learned with fierce disputes pursue,
And give to Titus old Vespasian's due.
    Ambition sighed: she found it vain to trust
The faithless column and the crumbling bust:
Huge moles, whose shadow stretched from shore to shore,
Their ruins perished, and their place no more;
Convinced, she now contracts her vast design,
And all her triumphs shrink into a coin.
A narrow orb each crowded conquest keeps;
Beneath her palm here sad Judea weeps;
Now scantier limits the proud arch confine,
And scarce are seen the prostrate Nile or Rhine;
A small Euphrates through the piece is rolled,
And little eagles wave their wings in gold.
The medal, faithful to its charge of fame,
Through climes and ages bears each form and name:
In one short view subjected to our eye
Gods, emperors, heroes, sages, beauties, lie.

With sharpened sight pale antiquaries pore,
The inscription value, but the rust adore.
This the blue varnish, that the green endears,
The sacred rust of twice ten hundred years!
To gain Pescennius one employs his schemes,
One grasps a Cecrops in ecstatic dreams.
Poor Vadius, long with learned spleen devoured,
Can taste no pleasure since his shield was scoured;
And Curio, restless by the fair one's side,
Sighs for an Otho, and neglects his bride.
  Theirs is the vanity, the learning thine:
Touched by thy hand, again Rome's glories shine;
Her gods and god-like heroes rise to view,
And all her faded garlands bloom anew.
Nor blush, these studies thy regard engage;
These pleased the fathers of poetic rage;
The verse and sculpture bore an equal part,
And art reflected images to art.
  Oh, when shall Britain, conscious of her claim,
Stand emulous of Greek and Roman fame?
In living medals see her wars enrolled,
And vanquished realms supply recording gold?
Here, rising bold, the patriot's honest face;
There warriors frowning in historic brass?
Then future ages with delight shall see
How Plato's, Bacon's, Newton's looks agree;
Or in fair series laurelled bards be shown,
A Virgil there, and here an Addison.
Then shall thy Craggs (and let me call him mine)
On the cast ore, another Pollio shine;
With aspect open, shall erect his head,
And round the orb in lasting notes be read,
"Statesmen, yet friend to truth! of soul sincere,

In action faithful, and in honour clear;
Who broke no promise, served no private end,
Who gained no title and who lost no friend;
Ennobled by himself, by all approved,
And praised, unenvied, by the muse he loved."

SATIRES.

EPISTLE TO DR. ARBUTHNOT.

ADVERTISEMENT
To the first publication of this Epistle.

This Paper is a sort of bill of complaint, begun many years since, and drawn up by snatches, as the several occasions offered. I had no thoughts of publishing it, till it pleased some persons of rank and fortune (the authors of "Verses to the Imitator of Horace," and of an "Epistle to a Doctor of Divinity from a Nobleman at Hampton Court") to attack, in a very extraordinary manner, not only my writings (of which, being public, the public is judge), but my person, morals, and family, whereof, to those who know me not, a truer information may be requisite. Being divided between the necessity to say something of myself, and my own laziness to undertake so awkward a task, I thought it the shortest way to put the last hand to this Epistle. If it have anything pleasing, it will be that by which I am most desirous to please, the truth and the sentiment; and if anything offensive, it will be only to those I am least sorry to offend, the vicious or the ungenerous.

Many will know their own pictures in it, there being not a circumstance but what is true; but I have, for the most part, spared their names, and they may escape being laughed at if they please.

I would have some of them know, it was owing to the request of the learned and candid friend to whom it is inscribed, that I make not as free use of theirs as they have done of mine. However, I shall have this advantage and honour on my side, that whereas, by their proceeding, any abuse may be directed at any man, no injury can possibly be done by mine, since a nameless character can never be found out but by its truth and likeness.--P.

EPISTLE TO DR. ARBUTHNOT, BEING THE PROLOGUE TO THE SATIRES.

P. Shut, shut the door, good John! fatigued, I said,
Tie up the knocker, say I'm sick, I'm dead.
The dog-star rages! nay 'tis past a doubt,
All Bedlam, or Parnassus, is let out:
Fire in each eye, and papers in each hand,
They rave, recite, and madden round the land.
   What walls can guard me, or what shades can hide?
They pierce my thickets, through my grot they glide;
By land, by water, they renew the charge;
They stop the chariot, and they board the barge.
No place is sacred, not the Church is free;

Even Sunday shines no Sabbath Day to me;
Then from the Mint walks forth the man of rhyme,
Happy to catch me just at dinner-time.
  Is there a parson, much bemused in beer,
A maudlin poetess, a rhyming peer,
A clerk, foredoomed his father's soul to cross,
Who pens a stanza when he should engross?
Is there, who, locked from ink and paper, scrawls
With desperate charcoal round his darkened walls?
All fly to Twitenham, and in humble strain
Apply to me, to keep them mad or vain.
Arthur, whose giddy son neglects the laws,
Imputes to me and my damned works the cause:
Poor Cornus sees his frantic wife elope,
And curses wit, and poetry, and Pope.
  Friend to my life! (which did not you prolong,
The world had wanted many an idle song)
What drop or nostrum can this plague remove?
Or which must end me, a fool's wrath or love?
A dire dilemma! either way I'm sped,
If foes, they write, if friends, they read me dead.
Seized and tied down to judge, how wretched I!
Who can't be silent, and who will not lie.
To laugh, were want of goodness and of grace,
And to be grave, exceeds all power of face.
I sit with sad civility, I read
With honest anguish, and an aching head;
And drop at last, but in unwilling ears,
This saving counsel, "Keep your piece nine years."
  "Nine years!" cries he, who high in Drury Lane,
Lulled by soft zephyrs through the broken pane,
Rhymes ere he wakes, and prints before term ends,
Obliged by hunger, and request of friends:

"The piece, you think, is incorrect? why, take it,
I'm all submission, what you'd have it, make it."
   Three things another's modest wishes bound,
My friendship, and a prologue, and ten pound.
   Pitholeon sends to me: "You know his Grace,
I want a patron; ask him for a place."
'Pitholeon libelled me'--"but here's a letter
Informs you, sir, 'twas when he knew no better.
Dare you refuse him? Curll invites to dine,
He'll write a journal, or he'll turn divine."
   Bless me! a packet.--"'Tis a stranger sues,
A virgin tragedy, an orphan muse."
If I dislike it, "Furies, death and rage!"
If I approve, "Commend it to the stage."
There (thank my stars) my whole commission ends,
The players and I are, luckily, no friends,
Fired that the house reject him, "'Sdeath I'll print it,
And shame the fools--Your interest, sir, with Lintot!"
'Lintot, dull rogue! will think your price too much:'
"Not, sir, if you revise it, and retouch."
All my demurs but double his attacks;
At last he whispers, "Do; and we go snacks."
Glad of a quarrel, straight I clap the door,
Sir, let me see your works and you no more.
   'Tis sung, when Midas' ears began to spring
(Midas, a sacred person and a king),
His very minister who spied them first
(Some say his queen) was forced to speak, or burst.
And is not mine, my friend, a sorer case,
When every coxcomb perks them in my face?
A. Good friend, forbear! you deal in dangerous things.
I'd never name queens, ministers, or kings;
Keep close to ears, and those let asses prick;

'Tis nothing-- P. Nothing? if they bite and kick?
Out with it, Dunciad! let the secret pass,
That secret to each fool, that he's an ass:
The truth once told (and wherefore should we lie?)
The Queen of Midas slept, and so may I.
  You think this cruel? take it for a rule,
No creature smarts so little as a fool.
Let peals of laughter, Codrus! round thee break,
Thou unconcerned canst hear the mighty crack:
Pit, box, and gallery in convulsions hurled,
Thou stand'st unshook amidst a bursting world.
Who shames a scribbler? break one cobweb through,
He spins the slight, self-pleasing thread anew:
Destroy his fib or sophistry, in vain,
The creature's at his dirty work again,
Throned in the centre of his thin designs,
Proud of a vast extent of flimsy lines!
Whom have I hurt? has poet yet, or peer,
Lost the arched eyebrow, or Parnassian sneer?
And has not Colley still his lord, and w***e?
His butchers Henley, his free-masons Moore?
Does not one table Bavius still admit?
Still to one bishop Philips seem a wit?
Still Sappho-- A. Hold! for God's sake--you'll offend,
No names!--be calm!--learn prudence of a friend!
I too could write, and I am twice as tall;
But foes like these-- P. One flatterer's worse than all.
Of all mad creatures, if the learned are right,
It is the slaver kills, and not the bite.
A fool quite angry is quite innocent:
Alas! 'tis ten times worse when they repent.
  One dedicates in high heroic prose,
And ridicules beyond a hundred foes:

One from all Grubstreet will my fame defend,
And more abusive, calls himself my friend.
This prints my letters, that expects a bribe,
And others roar aloud, "Subscribe, subscribe."
  There are, who to my person pay their court:
I cough like Horace, and, though lean, am short,
Ammon's great son one shoulder had too high,
Such Ovid's nose, and "Sir! you have an eye"--
Go on, obliging creatures, make me see
All that disgraced my betters, met in me.
Say for my comfort, languishing in bed,
"Just so immortal Maro held his head:"
And when I die, be sure you let me know
Great Homer died three thousand years ago.
  Why did I write? what sin to me unknown
Dipped me in ink, my parents', or my own?
As yet a child, nor yet a fool to fame,
I lisped in numbers, for the numbers came.
I left no calling for this idle trade,
No duty broke, no father disobeyed.
The Muse but served to ease some friend, not wife,
To help me through this long disease, my life,
To second, Arbuthnot! thy art and care,
And teach the being you preserved, to bear.
  But why then publish? Granville the polite,
And knowing Walsh, would tell me I could write;
Well-natured Garth, inflamed with early praise;
And Congreve loved, and Swift endured my lays;
The courtly Talbot, Somers, Sheffield, read;
Even mitred Rochester would nod the head,
And St. John's self (great Dryden's friends before)
With open arms received one poet more.
Happy my studies, when by these approved!

Happier their author, when by these beloved!
From these the world will judge of men and books,
Not from the Burnets, Oldmixons, and Cookes.
  Soft were my numbers; who could take offence,
While pure description held the place of sense?
Like gentle Fanny's was my flowery theme,
A painted mistress, or a purling stream.
Yet then did Gildon draw his venal quill;--
I wished the man a dinner, and sat still.
Yet then did Dennis rave in furious fret;
I never answered--I was not in debt.
If want provoked, or madness made them print,
I waged no war with Bedlam or the Mint.
  Did some more sober critic come abroad;
If wrong, I smiled; if right, I kissed the rod.
Pains, reading, study, are their just pretence,
And all they want is spirit, taste, and sense.
Commas and points they set exactly right,
And 'twere a sin to rob them of their mite.
Yet ne'er one sprig of laurel graced these ribalds,
From slashing Bentley down to p---g Tibalds:
Each wight, who reads not, and but scans and spells,
Each word-catcher, that lives on syllables,
Even such small critics some regard may claim,
Preserved in Milton's or in Shakespeare's name.
Pretty! in amber to observe the forms
Of hairs, or straws, or dirt, or grubs, or worms!
The things, we know, are neither rich nor rare,
But wonder how the devil they got there.
  Were others angry: I excused them too;
Well might they rage, I gave them but their due.
A man's true merit 'tis not hard to find;
But each man's secret standard in his mind,

That casting-weight pride adds to emptiness,
This, who can gratify? for who can guess?
The bard whom pilfered pastorals renown,
Who turns a Persian tale for half a crown,
Just writes to make his barrenness appear,
And strains, from hard-bound brains, eight lines a year;
He, who still wanting, though he lives on theft,
Steals much, spends little, yet has nothing left:
And he, who now to sense, now nonsense leaning,
Means not, but blunders round about a meaning:
And he, whose fustian's so sublimely bad,
It is not poetry, but prose run mad:
All these, my modest satire bade translate,
And owned that nine such poets made a Tate.
How did they fume, and stamp, and roar, and chafe
And swear not Addison himself was safe.
  Peace to all such! but were there one whose fires
True genius kindles, and fair fame inspires;
Blessed with each talent and each art to please,
And born to write, converse, and live with ease:
Should such a man, too fond to rule alone,
Bear, like the Turk, no brother near the throne.
View him with scornful, yet with jealous eyes,
And hate for arts that caused himself to rise;
Damn with faint praise, assent with civil leer,
And without sneering, teach the rest to sneer;
Willing to wound, and yet afraid to strike,
Just hint a fault, and hesitate dislike;
Alike reserved to blame, or to commend,
A timorous foe, and a suspicious friend;
Dreading even fools, by flatterers besieged,
And so obliging, that he ne'er obliged;
Like Cato, give his little senate laws,

And sit attentive to his own applause;
While wits and templars every sentence raise,
And wonder with a foolish face of praise:--
Who but must laugh, if such a man there be?
Who would not weep, if Atticus were he?
  What though my name stood rubric on the walls,
Or plaistered posts, with claps, in capitals?
Or smoking forth, a hundred hawkers' load,
On wings of winds came flying all abroad?
I sought no homage from the race that write;
I kept, like Asian monarchs, from their sight:
Poems I heeded (now be-rhymed so long)
No more than thou, great George! a birthday song.
I ne'er with wits or witlings passed my days,
To spread about the itch of verse and praise;
Nor like a puppy, daggled through the town,
To fetch and carry sing-song up and down;
Nor at rehearsals sweat, and mouthed, and cried,
With handkerchief and orange at my side;
But sick of fops, and poetry, and prate,
To Bufo left the whole Castalian state.
  Proud as Apollo on his forked hill,
Sat full-blown Bufo puffed by every quill;
Fed with soft dedication all day long,
Horace and he went hand in hand in song.
His library (where busts of poets dead
And a true Pindar stood without a head)
Received of wits an undistinguished race,
Who first his judgment asked, and then a place:
Much they extolled his pictures, much his seat,
And flattered every day, and some days eat:
Till grown more frugal in his riper days,
He paid some bards with port, and some with praise;

To some a dry rehearsal was assigned,
And others (harder still) he paid in kind.
Dryden alone (what wonder?) came not nigh,
Dryden alone escaped this judging eye:
But still the great have kindness in reserve,
He helped to bury whom he helped to starve.
   May some choice patron bless each grey goose quill!
May every Bavius have his Bufo still!
So, when a statesman wants a day's defence,
Or envy holds a whole week's war with sense,
Or simple pride for flattery makes demands,
May dunce by dunce be whistled off my hands!
Blessed be the great! for those they take away,
And those they left me; for they left me gay;
Left me to see neglected genius bloom,
Neglected die, and tell it on his tomb:
Of all thy blameless life the soul return
My verse, and Queensbury weeping o'er thy urn!
   Oh let me live my own, and die so too!
(To live and die is all I have to do:)
Maintain a poet's dignity and ease,
And see what friends, and read what books I please;
Above a patron, though I condescend
Sometimes to call a minister my friend.
I was not born for courts or great affairs;
I pay my debts, believe, and say my prayers;
Can sleep without a poem in my head;
Nor know, if Dennis be alive or dead.
   Why am I asked what next shall see the light?
Heavens! was I born for nothing but to write?
Has life no joys for me! or (to be grave)
Have I no friend to serve, no soul to save?
"I found him close with Swift."--'Indeed? no doubt,'

(Cries prating Balbus) 'something will come out.'
'Tis all in vain, deny it as I will.
'No, such a genius never can lie still;'
And then for mine obligingly mistakes
The first lampoon Sir Will. or Bubo makes.
Poor guiltless I! and can I choose but smile
When every coxcomb knows me by my style?
   Cursed be the verse, how well soe'er it flow
That tends to make one worthy man my foe,
Give virtue scandal, innocence a fear,
Or from the soft-eyed virgin steal a tear!
But he who hurts a harmless neighbour's peace,
Insults fallen worth, or beauty in distress,
Who loves a lie, lame slander helps about,
Who writes a libel, or who copies out:
That fop, whose pride affects a patron's name,
Yet absent, wounds an author's honest fame:
Who can your merit selfishly approve,
And show the sense of it without the love;
Who has the vanity to call you friend,
Yet wants the honour, injured, to defend;
Who tells whate'er you think, whate'er you say,
And, if he lie not, must at least betray:
Who to the Dean, and silver bell can swear,
And sees at Canons what was never there;
Who reads, but with a lust to misapply,
Make satire a lampoon, and fiction, lie.
A lash like mine no honest man shall dread,
But all such babbling blockheads in his stead.
   Let Sporus tremble-- A. What? that thing of silk,
Sporus, that mere white curd of ass's milk,
Satire or sense, alas! can Sporus feel?
Who breaks a butterfly upon a wheel?

P. Yet let me flap this bug with gilded wings,
This painted child of dirt, that stinks and stings;
Whose buzz the witty and the fair annoys,
Yet wit ne'er tastes, and beauty ne'er enjoys:
So well-bred spaniels civilly delight
In mumbling of the game they dare not bite:
Eternal smiles his emptiness betray,
As shallow streams run dimpling all the way.
Whether in florid impotence he speaks
And, as the prompter breathes, the puppet squeaks;
Or at the ear of Eve, familiar toad,
Half froth, half venom, spits himself abroad,
In puns, or politics, or tales, or lies,
Or spite, or smut, or rhymes, or blasphemies.
His wit all see-saw, between that and this, }
Now high, now low, now master up, now miss, }
And he himself one vile antithesis. }
Amphibious thing! that acting either part,
The trifling head or the corrupted heart,
Fop at the toilet, flatterer at the board,
Now trips a lady, and now struts a lord.
Eve's tempter thus the rabbins have expressed,
A cherub's face, a reptile all the rest;
Beauty that shocks you, parts that none will trust;
Wit that can creep, and pride that licks the dust.
  Not fortunes worshipper, nor fashion's fool,
Not lucre's madman, nor ambition's tool,
Not proud, nor servile;--be one poet's praise,
That, if he pleased, he pleased by manly ways:
That flattery, even to kings, he held a shame,
And thought a lie in verse or prose the same.
That not in fancy's maze he wandered long:
But stooped to truth, and moralised his song:

That not for fame, but virtue's better end,
He stood the furious foe, the timid friend,
The damning critic, half approving wit,
The coxcomb hit, or fearing to be hit;
Laughed at the loss of friends he never had,
The dull, the proud, the wicked, and the mad;
The distant threats of vengeance on his head,
The blow unfelt, the tear he never shed;
The tale revived, the lie so oft o'erthrown,
The imputed trash, and dulness not his own;
The morals blackened when the writings scape,
The libelled person, and the pictured shape;
Abuse, on all he loved, or loved him, spread,
A friend in exile, or a father, dead;
The whisper, that to greatness still too near,
Perhaps, yet vibrates, on his sovereign's ear:--
Welcome for thee, fair virtue! all the past;
For thee, fair virtue! welcome even the last!
    A. But why insult the poor, affront the great?
    P. A knave's a knave, to me in every state:
Alike my scorn, if he succeed or fail,
Sporus at Court, or Japhet in a jail,
A hireling scribbler, or a hireling peer,
Knight of the post corrupt, or of the shire;
If on a pillory, or near a throne,
He gain his prince's ear, or lose his own.
    Yet soft by nature, more a dupe than wit,
Sappho can tell you how this man was bit;
This dreaded satirist Dennis will confess
Foe to his pride, but friend to his distress:
So humble, he has knocked at Tibbald's door,
Has drunk with Cibber, nay has rhymed for Moore.
Full ten years slandered, did he once reply?

Three thousand sons went down on Welsted's lie.
To please a mistress one aspersed his life;
He lashed him not, but let her be his wife.
Let Budgel charge low Grubstreet on his quill,
And write whate'er he pleased, except his will;
Let the two Curlls of town and court abuse
His father, mother, body, soul, and muse.
Yet why? that father held it for a rule,
It was a sin to call our neighbour fool:
That harmless mother thought no wife a w***e:
Hear this, and spare his family, James Moore!
Unspotted names, and memorable long!
If there be force in virtue, or in song.

   Of gentle blood (part shed in honour's cause
While yet in Britain honour had applause)
Each parent sprung-- A. What fortune, pray?-- P. Their own,
And better got, than Bestia's from the throne.
Born to no pride, inheriting no strife,
Nor marrying discord in a noble wife,
Stranger to civil and religious rage,
The good man walked innoxious through his age.
Nor courts he saw, no suits would ever try,
Nor dared an oath, nor hazarded a lie.
Unlearned he knew no schoolman's subtle art,
No language, but the language of the heart.
By nature honest, by experience wise,
Healthy by temperance, and by exercise;
His life, though long, to sickness past unknown,
His death was instant, and without a groan.
O grant me thus to live, and thus to die!
Who sprung from kings shall know less joy than I.

   O friend! may each domestic bliss be thine!
Be no unpleasing melancholy mine:

Me, let the tender office long engage,
To rock the cradle of reposing age,
With lenient arts extend a mother's breath,
Make languor smile, and smooth the bed of death,
Explore the thought, explain the asking eye,
And keep a while one parent from the sky!
On cares like these if length of days attend,
May Heaven, to bless those days, preserve my friend,
Preserve him social, cheerful, and serene,
And just as rich as when he served a queen.
   A. Whether that blessing be denied or given,
Thus far was right, the rest belongs to Heaven.

SATIRES AND EPISTLES OF HORACE IMITATED.

ADVERTISEMENT.

The occasion of publishing these Imitations was the clamour raised on
some of my Epistles. An answer from Horace was both more full, and of
more dignity, than any I could have made in my own person; and the
example of much greater freedom in so eminent a divine as Dr. Donne,
seemed a proof with what indignation and contempt a Christian may treat
vice or folly, in ever so low, or ever so high a station. Both these
authors were acceptable to the princes and ministers under whom they
lived. The Satires of Dr. Donne I versified, at the desire of the Earl
of Oxford while he was Lord Treasurer, and of the Duke of Shrewsbury
who
had been Secretary of State, neither of whom looked upon a satire on
vicious courts as any reflection on those they served in. And indeed

there is not in the world a greater error, than that which fools are so
apt to fall into, and knaves with good reason to encourage, the mistaking
a satirist for a libeller; whereas to a true satirist nothing is so
odious as a libeller, for the same reason as to a man truly virtuous
nothing is so hateful as a hypocrite.

Uni aequus Virtuti atque ejus Amicis. P.

THE FIRST SATIRE OF THE
SECOND BOOK OF HORACE.

SATIRE I. TO MR. FORTESCUE.

   P. There are (I scarce can think it, but am told),
There are, to whom my satire seems too bold:
Scarce to wise Peter complaisant enough,
And something said of Chartres much too rough.
The lines are weak another's pleased to say,
Lord Fanny spins a thousand such a day.
Timorous by nature, of the rich in awe,
I come to counsel learned in the law:
You'll give me, like a friend both sage and free,
Advice; and (as you use) without a fee.
   F. I'd write no more. P. Not write? but then I think,
And for my soul I cannot sleep a wink.
I nod in company, I wake at night,
Fools rush into my head, and so I write.
   F. You could not do a worse thing for your life.

Why, if the nights seem tedious--take a wife:
Or rather truly, if your point be rest,
Lettuce and cowslip wine: Probatum est.
But talk with Celsus, Celsus will advise
Hartshorn, or something that shall close your eyes.
Or, if you needs must write, write Caesar's praise,
You'll gain at least a knighthood, or the bays.

   P. What? like Sir Richard, rumbling, rough, and fierce,
With arms, and George, and Brunswick crowd the verse,
Rend with tremendous sound your ears asunder,
With gun, drum, trumpet, blunderbuss, and thunder?
Or nobly wild, with Budgel's fire and force,
Paint angels trembling round his falling horse?

   F. Then all your muse's softer art display,
Let Carolina smooth the tuneful lay,
Lull with Amelia's liquid name the nine,
And sweetly flow through all the royal line.

   P. Alas! few verses touch their nicer ear;
They scarce can bear their laureate twice a year;
And justly Caesar scorns the poet's lays:
It is to history he trusts for praise.

   F. Better be Cibber, I'll maintain it still,
Than ridicule all taste, blaspheme quadrille,
Abuse the city's best good men in metre,
And laugh at peers that put their trust in Peter.
Even those you touch not, hate you. P. What should ail 'em?

   F. A hundred smart in Timon and in Balaam:
The fewer still you name, you wound the more;
Bond is but one, but Harpax is a score.

   P. Each mortal has his pleasure: none deny
Scarsdale his bottle, Darty his ham-pie;
Ridotta sips and dances, till she see
The doubling lustres dance as fast as she;

F---- loves the senate, Hockley-hole his brother,
Like in all else, as one egg to another.
I love to pour out all myself, as plain
As downright Shippen, or as old Montaigne:
In them, as certain to be loved as seen,
The soul stood forth, nor kept a thought within;
In me what spots (for spots I have) appear,
Will prove at least the medium must be clear.
In this impartial glass, my muse intends
Fair to expose myself, my foes, my friends;
Publish the present age; but where my text
Is vice too high, reserve it for the next:
My foes shall wish my life a longer date,
And every friend the less lament my fate.
My head and heart thus flowing through my quill,
Verse-man or prose-man, term me which you will,
Papist or Protestant, or both between,
Like good Erasmus in an honest mean,
In moderation placing all my glory,
While Tories call me Whig, and Whigs a Tory.
  Satire's my weapon, but I'm too discreet
To run a muck, and tilt at all I meet;
I only wear it in a land of Hectors,
Thieves, supercargoes, sharpers, and directors.
Save but our army! and let Jove encrust
Swords, pikes, and guns, with everlasting rust!
Peace is my dear delight--not Fleury's more:
But touch me, and no minister so sore.
Whoe'er offends, at some unlucky time
Slides into verse, and hitches in a rhyme,
Sacred to ridicule his whole life long,
And the sad burthen of some merry song.
  Slander or poison dread from Delia's rage

Hard words or hanging, if your judge be Page.
From furious Sappho scarce a milder fate,
Plagued by her love, or libelled by her hate.
Its proper power to hurt, each creature feels;
Bulls aim their horns, and asses lift their heels;
'Tis a bear's talent not to kick, but hug;
And no man wonders he's not stung by pug.
So drink with Walters, or with Chartres eat,
They'll never poison you, they'll only cheat.

   Then, learned sir! (to cut the matter short)
Whate'er my fate, or well or ill at Court,
Whether old age, with faint but cheerful ray,
Attends to gild the evening of my day,
Or death's black wing already be displayed,
To wrap me in the universal shade;
Whether the darkened room to muse invite,
Or whitened wall provoke the skewer to write:
In durance, exile, Bedlam or the Mint--
Like Lee or Budgel, I will rhyme and print.

   F. Alas, young man! your days can ne'er be long,
In flower of age you perish for a song!
Plums and directors, Shylock and his wife,
Will club their testers, now, to take your life!

   P. What? armed for virtue when I point the pen,
Brand the bold front of shameless guilty men;
Dash the proud gamester in his gilded car;
Bare the mean heart that lurks beneath a star;
Can there be wanting, to defend her cause,
Lights of the Church, or guardians of the laws?
Could pensioned Boileau lash in honest strain
Flatterers and bigots even in Louis' reign?
Could Laureate Dryden pimp and friar engage,
Yet neither Charles nor James be in a rage?

And I not strip the gilding off a knave,
Unplaced, unpensioned, no man's heir, or slave?
I will, or perish in the generous cause:
Hear this, and tremble! you, who 'scape the laws.
Yes, while I live, no rich or noble knave
Shall walk the world, in credit, to his grave.
To Virtue only and her friends a friend,
The world beside may murmur, or commend.
Know, all the distant din that world can keep
Rolls o'er my grotto, and but soothes my sleep.
There, my retreat the best companions grace,
Chiefs out of war, and statesmen out of place.
There St. John mingles with my friendly bowl
The feast of reason and the flow of soul:
And he, whose lightning pierced the Iberian lines,
Now forms my quincunx, and now ranks my vines
Or tames the genius of the stubborn plain,
Almost as quickly as he conquered Spain.

   Envy must own, I live among the great,
No pimp of pleasure, and no spy of state.
With eyes that pry not, tongue that ne'er repeats,
Fond to spread friendships, but to cover heats;
To help who want, to forward who excel;
This, all who know me, know; who love me, tell;
And who unknown defame me, let them be
Scribblers or peers, alike are mob to me.
This is my plea, on this I rest my cause--
What saith my counsel, learned in the laws?

   F. Your plea is good; but still I say, beware!
Laws are explained by men--so have a care.
It stands on record, that in Richard's times
A man was hanged for very honest rhymes.
Consult the Statute: quart. I think it is,

Edwardi sext. or prim. et quint. Eliz.
See libels, satires--here you have it--read.
   P. Libels and satires! lawless things indeed!
But grave epistles, bringing vice to light,
Such as a king might read, a bishop write;
Such as Sir Robert would approve-- F. Indeed?
The case is altered--you may then proceed;
In such a cause the plaintiff would be hissed;
My lords the judges laugh, and you're dismissed.

THE SECOND SATIRE OF THE SECOND BOOK OF HORACE.

SATIRE II. TO MR. BETHEL.

What, and how great, the virtue and the art
To live on little with a cheerful heart
(A doctrine sage, but truly none of mine),
Let's talk, my friends, but talk before we dine.
Not when a gilt buffet's reflected pride
Turns you from sound philosophy aside;
Not when from plate to plate your eyeballs roll,
And the brain dances to the mantling bowl.
   Hear Bethel's sermon, one not versed in schools,
But strong in sense, and wise without the rules.
   Go work, hunt, exercise! (he thus began)
Then scorn a homely dinner, if you can.
Your wine locked up, your butler strolled abroad,

Or fish denied (the river yet unthawed),
If then plain bread and milk will do the feat,
The pleasure lies in you, and not the meat.
   Preach as I please, I doubt our curious men
Will choose a pheasant still before a hen;
Yet hens of Guinea full as good I hold,
Except you eat the feathers green and gold.
Of carps and mullets why prefer the great
(Though cut in pieces ere my lord can eat),
Yet for small turbots such esteem profess?
Because God made these large, the other less.
   Oldfield with more than harpy throat endued,
Cries "Send me, gods! a whole hog barbecued!
Oh, b---- it, south-winds! till a stench exhale
Rank as the ripeness of a rabbit's tail.
By what criterion do ye eat, d'ye think,
If this is prized for sweetness, that for stink?"
When the tired glutton labours through a treat,
He finds no relish in the sweetest meat,
He calls for something bitter, something sour,
And the rich feast concludes extremely poor:
Cheap eggs, and herbs, and olives still we see;
Thus much is left of old simplicity!
The robin-redbreast till of late had rest,
And children sacred held a martin's nest,
Till becca-ficos sold so devilish dear
To one that was, or would have been a peer.
Let me extol a cat, on oysters fed,
I'll have a party at the Bedford-head;
Or even to crack live crawfish recommend;
I'd never doubt at Court to make a friend.
   'Tis yet in vain, I own, to keep a pother
About one vice, and fall into the other:

Between excess and famine lies a mean;
Plain, but not sordid; though not splendid, clean.
  Avidien, or his wife (no matter which,
For him you'll call a dog, and her a bitch)
Sell their presented partridges, and fruits,
And humbly live on rabbits and on roots:
One half-pint bottle serves them both to dine,
And is at once their vinegar and wine.
But on some lucky day (as when they found
A lost bank-bill, or heard their son was drowned)
At such a feast, old vinegar to spare,
Is what two souls so generous cannot bear:
Oil, though it stink, they drop by drop impart,
But souse the cabbage with a bounteous heart.
  He knows to live, who keeps the middle state,
And neither leans on this side, nor on that;
Nor stops, for one bad cork, his butler's pay,
Swears, like Albutius, a good cook away;
Nor lets, like Naevius, every error pass,
The musty wine, foul cloth, or greasy glass.
  Now hear what blessings temperance can bring:
(Thus said our friend, and what he said I sing,)
First health: The stomach (crammed from every dish,
A tomb of boiled and roast, and flesh and fish,
Where bile, and wind, and phlegm, and acid jar,
And all the man is one intestine war)
Remembers oft the schoolboy's simple fare,
The temperate sleeps, and spirits light as air.
  How pale, each worshipful and reverend guest
Rise from a clergy, or a city feast!
What life in all that ample body, say?
What heavenly particle inspires the clay?
The soul subsides, and wickedly inclines

To seem but mortal, even in sound divines.
   On morning wings how active springs the mind
That leaves the load of yesterday behind!
How easy every labour it pursues!
How coming to the poet every muse!
Not but we may exceed, some holy time,
Or tired in search of truth, or search of rhyme;
Ill health some just indulgence may engage,
And more the sickness of long life, old age;
For fainting age what cordial drop remains,
If our intemperate youth the vessel drains?
   Our fathers praised rank venison. You suppose,
Perhaps, young men! our fathers had no nose.
Not so: a buck was then a week's repast,
And 'twas their point, I ween, to make it last;
More pleased to keep it till their friends could come,
Than eat the sweetest by themselves at home.
Why had not I in those good times my birth,
Ere coxcomb pies or coxcombs were on earth?
   Unworthy he, the voice of fame to hear,
That sweetest music to an honest ear;
(For 'faith, Lord Fanny! you are in the wrong
The world's good word is better than a song)
Who has not learned fresh sturgeon and ham-pie
Are no rewards for want, and infamy?
When luxury has licked up all thy pelf,
Cursed by thy neighbours, thy trustees, thyself,
To friends, to fortune, to mankind a shame,
Think how posterity will treat thy name;
And buy a rope, that future times may tell,
Thou hast at least bestowed one penny well.
   "Right," cries his lordship, "for a rogue in need
To have a taste is insolence indeed:

In me 'tis noble, suits my birth and state,
My wealth unwieldy, and my heap too great."
Then, like the sun, let bounty spread her ray,
And shine that superfluity away.
Oh, impudence of wealth! with all thy store,
How dar'st thou let one worthy man be poor?
Shall half the new-built churches round thee fall?
Make quays, build bridges, or repair Whitehall:
Or to thy country let that heap be lent,
As M**o's was, but not at five per cent.
   Who thinks that Fortune cannot change her mind,
Prepares a dreadful jest for all mankind.
And who stands safest? tell me, is it he
That spreads and swells in puffed posterity,
Or blest with little, whose preventing care
In peace provides fit arms against a war?
   Thus Bethel spoke, who always speaks his thought,
And always thinks the very thing he ought:
His equal mind I copy what I can,
And, as I love, would imitate the man.
In South-Sea days not happier, when surmised
The lord of thousands, than if now excised;
In forest planted by a father's hand,
Than in five acres now of rented land.
Content with little, I can p----e here
On broccoli and mutton, round the year;
But ancient friends (though poor, or out of play)
That touch my bell, I cannot turn away.
'Tis true, no turbots dignify my boards,
But gudgeons, flounders, what my Thames affords:
To Hounslow Heath I point and Banstead Down,
Thence comes your mutton, and these chicks my own:
From yon old walnut-tree a shower shall fall;

And grapes, long lingering on my only wall,
And figs from standard and espalier join;
The devil is in you if you cannot dine:
Then cheerful healths (your mistress shall have place),
And, what's more rare, a poet shall say grace.
  Fortune not much of humbling me can boast;
Though double taxed, how little have I lost?
My life's amusements have been just the same,
Before, and after, standing armies came.
My lands are sold, my father's house is gone;
I'll hire another's; is not that my own,
And yours, my friends? through whose free-opening gate
None comes too early, none departs too late;
(For I, who hold sage Homer's rule the best,
Welcome the coming, speed the going guest).
"Pray Heaven it last!" (cries Swift!) "as you go on;
I wish to God this house had been your own:
Pity! to build without a son or wife:
Why, you'll enjoy it only all your life."
Well, if the use be mine, can it concern one,
Whether the name belong to Pope or Vernon?
What's property? dear Swift! you see it alter
From you to me, from me to Peter Walter;
Or, in a mortgage, prove a lawyer's share;
Or, in a jointure, vanish from the heir;
Or in pure equity (the case not clear)
The Chancery takes your rents for twenty year:
At best, it falls to some ungracious son,
Who cries, "My father's damned, and all's my own."
Shades, that to Bacon could retreat afford,
Become the portion of a booby lord;
And Hemsley, once proud Buckingham's delight,
Slides to a scrivener or a city knight.

Let lands and houses have what lords they will,
Let us be fixed, and our own masters still.

THE FIRST EPISTLE OF THE
FIRST BOOK OF HORACE.

EPISTLE I. TO LORD BOLINGBROKE.

  St. John, whose love indulged my labours past,
Matures my present, and shall bound my last!
Why will you break the Sabbath of my days?
Now sick alike of envy and of praise.
Public too long, ah let me hide my age!
See, modest Cibber now has left the stage:
Our generals now, retired to their estates,
Hang their old trophies o'er the garden gates,
In life's cool evening satiate of applause,
Nor fond of bleeding, even in Brunswick's cause.
  A voice there is, that whispers in my ear,
('Tis Reason's voice, which sometimes one can hear)
"Friend Pope, be prudent, let your muse take breath,
And never gallop Pegasus to death;
Lest stiff and stately, void of fire or force,
You limp, like Blackmore, on a lord mayor's horse."
  Farewell then verse, and love, and every toy,
The rhymes and rattles of the man or boy;
What right, what true, what fit we justly call,
Let this be all my care--for this is all.

To lay this harvest up, and hoard with haste
What every day will want, and most, the last.
    But ask not, to what doctors I apply?
Sworn to no master, of no sect am I:
As drives the storm, at any door I knock:
And house with Montaigne now, or now with Locke.
Sometimes a patriot, active in debate,
Mix with the world, and battle for the State,
Free as young Lyttelton, her cause pursue,
Still true to virtue, and as warm as true:
Sometimes with Aristippus, or St. Paul,
Indulge my candour, and grow all to all;
Back to my native moderation slide,
And win my way by yielding to the tide.
 Long, as to him who works for debt, the day,
Long as the night to her whose love's away,
Long as the year's dull circle seems to run,
When the brisk minor pants for twenty-one:
So slow th' unprofitable moments roll,
That lock up all the functions of my soul;
That keep me from myself; and still delay
Life's instant business to a future day:
That task, which as we follow, or despise,
The eldest is a fool, the youngest wise;
Which done, the poorest can no wants endure;
And which not done, the richest must be poor.
    Late as it is, I put myself to school,
And feel some comfort, not to be a fool.
Weak though I am of limb, and short of sight,
Far from a lynx, and not a giant quite;
I'll do what Mead and Cheselden advise,
To keep these limbs, and to preserve these eyes.
Not to go back, is somewhat to advance,

And men must walk at least before they dance.
  Say, does thy blood rebel, thy bosom move
With wretched avarice, or as wretched love?
Know, there are words and spells, which can control
Between the fits this fever of the soul:
Know, there are rhymes, which fresh and fresh applied
Will cure the arrant'st puppy of his pride.
Be furious, envious, slothful, mad, or drunk,
Slave to a wife, or vassal to a punk,
A Switz, a High Dutch, or a Low Dutch bear;
All that we ask is but a patient ear.
  'Tis the first virtue, vices to abhor;
And the first wisdom, to be fool no more.
But to the world no bugbear is so great,
As want of figure, and a small estate.
To either India see the merchant fly,
Scared at the spectre of pale poverty!
See him, with pains of body, pangs of soul,
Burn through the Tropic, freeze beneath the pole!
Wilt thou do nothing for a nobler end,
Nothing, to make philosophy thy friend?
To stop thy foolish views, thy long desires,
And ease thy heart of all that it admires?
  Here, wisdom calls: "Seek virtue first, be bold!
As gold to silver, virtue is to gold."
There, London's voice: "Get money, money still!
And then let virtue follow, if she will."
This, this the saving doctrine, preached to all,
From low St. James's up to high St. Paul;
From him whose quills stand quivered at his ear,
To him who notches sticks at Westminster.
  Barnard in spirit, sense, and truth abounds;
"Pray then, what wants he?" fourscore thousand pounds;

A pension, or such harness for a slave
As Bug now has, and Dorimant would have.
Barnard, thou art a Cit, with all thy worth;
But Bug and D * l, their honours, and so forth.
    Yet every child another song will sing:
"Virtue, brave boys! 'tis virtue makes a king."
True, conscious honour is to feel no sin,
He's armed without that's innocent within;
Be this thy screen, and this thy wall of brass;
Compared to this, a minister's an ass.
    And say, to which shall our applause belong,
This new Court jargon, or the good old song?
The modern language of corrupted peers,
Or what was spoke at Cressy and Poitiers?
Who counsels best? who whispers, "Be but great,
With praise or infamy leave that to fate;
Get place and wealth, if possible, with grace;
If not, by any means get wealth and place--"
For what? to have a box where eunuchs sing,
And foremost in the circle eye a king.
Or he, who bids thee face with steady view }
Proud fortune, and look shallow greatness through: }
And, while he bids thee, sets th' example too? }
If such a doctrine, in St. James's air,
Should chance to make the well-dressed rabble stare;
If honest S * z take scandal at a spark,
That less admires the palace than the park:
Faith I shall give the answer Reynard gave:
"I cannot like, dread sir, your royal cave:
Because I see, by all the tracks about,
Full many a beast goes in, but none come out."
Adieu to virtue, if you're once a slave:
Send her to Court, you send her to her grave.

Well, if a king's a lion, at the least,
The people are a many-headed beast:
Can they direct what measures to pursue,
Who know themselves so little what to do?
Alike in nothing but one lust of gold,
Just half the land would buy, and half be sold:
Their country's wealth our mightier misers drain,
Or cross, to plunder provinces, the main;
The rest, some farm the poor-box, some the pews;
Some keep assemblies, and would keep the stews;
Some with fat bucks on childless dotards fawn;
Some win rich widows by their chine and brawn;
While with the silent growth of ten per cent.
In dirt and darkness, hundreds stink content.

Of all these ways, if each pursues his own,
Satire be kind, and let the wretch alone:
But show me one who has it in his power
To act consistent with himself an hour.
Sir Job sailed forth, the evening bright and still,
"No place on earth," he cried, "like Greenwich Hill!"
Up starts a palace; lo, th' obedient base }
Slopes at its foot, the woods its sides embrace, }
The silver Thames reflects its marble face. }
Now let some whimsy, or that devil within }
Which guides all those who know not what they mean, }
But give the knight (or give his lady) spleen; }
"Away, away! take all your scaffolds down,
For snug's the word: my dear! we'll live in town."

At amorous Flavio is the stocking thrown?
That very night he longs to lie alone.
The fool, whose wife elopes some thrice a quarter,
For matrimonial solace dies a martyr.
Did ever Proteus, Merlin, any witch, }

Transform themselves so strangely as the rich? }
Well, but the poor--the poor have the same itch; }
They change their weekly barber, weekly news,
Prefer a new japanner to their shoes,
Discharge their garrets, move their beds, and run
(They know not whither) in a chaise and one;
They hire their sculler, and when once aboard,
Grow sick, and damn the climate--like a lord.
  You laugh, half beau, half sloven if I stand,
My wig all powder, and all snuff my band;
You laugh, if coat and breeches strangely vary,
White gloves, and linen worthy Lady Mary!
But when no prelate's lawn with hair-shirt lined,
Is half so incoherent as my mind,
When (each opinion with the next at strife,
One ebb and flow of follies all my life)
I plant, root up; I build, and then confound;
Turn round to square, and square again to round;
You never change one muscle of your face,
You think this madness but a common case,
Nor once to Chancery, nor to Hale apply;
Yet hang your lip, to see a seam awry!
Careless how ill I with myself agree,
Kind to my dress, my figure, not to me.
Is this my guide, philosopher, and Friend?
This, he who loves me, and who ought to mend?
Who ought to make me (what he can, or none),
That man divine whom wisdom calls her own;
Great without title, without fortune blessed;
Rich even when plundered, honoured while oppressed;
Loved without youth, and followed without power;
At home, though exiled; free, though in the Tower;
In short, that reasoning, high, immortal thing,

Just less than Jove, and much above a king,
Nay, half in heaven--except (what's mighty odd)
A fit of vapours clouds this demi-god.

THE SIXTH EPISTLE OF THE FIRST BOOK OF HORACE.

EPISTLE VI. TO MR. MURRAY.

"Not to admire, is all the art I know,
To make men happy, and to keep them so."
(Plain truth, dear Murray, needs no flowers of speech,
So take it in the very words of Creech.)
This vault of air, this congregated ball,
Self-centred sun, and stars that rise and fall,
There are, my friend! whose philosophic eyes
Look through, and trust the ruler with his skies,
To him commit the hour, the day, the year,
And view this dreadful all without a fear.
Admire we, then, what earth's low entrails hold, }
Arabian shores, or Indian seas infold. }
All the mad trade of fools and slaves for gold? }
Or popularity? or stars and strings?
The mob's applauses, or the gifts of kings?
Say with what eyes we ought at courts to gaze,
And pay the great our homage of amaze?
    If weak the pleasure that from these can spring,
The fear to want them is as weak a thing:

Whether we dread, or whether we desire,
In either case, believe me, we admire;
Whether we joy or grieve, the same the curse,
Surprised at better, or surprised at worse.
Thus good or bad, to one extreme betray
Th' unbalanced mind, and snatch the man away;
For virtue's self may too much zeal be had;
The worst of madmen is a saint run mad.
    Go then, and if you can, admire the state
Of beaming diamonds, and reflected plate;
Procure a taste to double the surprise,
And gaze on Parian charms with learned eyes:
Be struck with bright brocade, or Tyrian dye,
Our birthday nobles' splendid livery.
If not so pleased, at council-board rejoice,
To see their judgments hang upon thy voice;
From morn to night, at senate, rolls, and hall,
Plead much, read more, dine late, or not at all.
But wherefore all this labour, all this strife?
For fame, for riches, for a noble wife?
Shall one whom nature, learning, birth, conspired
To form not to admire but be admired,
Sigh, while his Chloe blind to wit and worth
Weds the rich dulness of some son of earth?
Yet time ennobles, or degrades each line;
It brightened Craggs's, and may darken thine:
And what is fame? the meanest have their day,
The greatest can but blaze and pass away.
Graced as thou art, with all the power of words,
So known, so honoured, at the House of Lords:
Conspicuous scene! another yet is nigh,
(More silent far) where kings and poets lie;
Where Murray (long enough his country's pride)

Shall be no more than Tully, or than Hyde!
  Racked with sciatics, martyred with the stone,
Will any mortal let himself alone?
See Ward by battered beaux invited over,
And desperate misery lays hold on Dover.
The case is easier in the mind's disease;
There all men may be cured, whene'er they please,
Would ye be blest? despise low joys, low gains; }
Disdain whatever Cornbury disdains; }
Be virtuous and be happy for your pains. }
  But art thou one, whom new opinions sway,
One who believes as Tindal leads the way,
Who virtue and a church alike disowns,
Thinks that but words, and this but brick and stones?
Fly then on all the wings of wild desire,
Admire whate'er the maddest can admire.
Is wealth thy passion? Hence! from pole to pole,
Where winds can carry, or where waves can roll,
For Indian spices, for Peruvian gold,
Prevent the greedy, and out-bid the bold:
Advance thy golden mountain to the skies;
On the broad base of fifty thousand rise,
Add one round hundred, and (if that's not fair)
Add fifty more, and bring it to a square.
For, mark th' advantage; just so many score
Will gain a wife with half as many more,
Procure her beauty, make that beauty chaste,
And then such friends--as cannot fail to last.
A man of wealth is dubbed a man of worth,
Venus shall give him form, and Antis birth.
(Believe me, many a German Prince is worse,
Who proud of pedigree, is poor of purse.)
His wealth brave Timon gloriously confounds;

Asked for a groat, he gives a hundred pounds;
Or if three ladies like a luckless play,
Takes the whole house upon the poet's day.
Now, in such exigencies not to need,
Upon my word, you must be rich indeed;
A noble superfluity it craves,
Not for yourself, but for your fools and knaves:
Something, which for your honour they may cheat,
And which it much becomes you to forget.
If wealth alone then make and keep us blest,
Still, still be getting, never, never rest.

 But if to power and place your passion lie,
If in the pomp of life consist the joy;
Then hire a slave, or (if you will) a lord
To do the honours, and to give the word;
Tell at your levee, as the crowds approach,
To whom to nod, whom take into your coach,
Whom honour with your hand: to make remarks,
Who rules in Cornwall, or who rules in Berks:
"This may be troublesome, is near the chair;
That makes three members, this can choose a mayor."
Instructed thus, you bow, embrace, protest, }
Adopt him son, or cousin at the least, }
Then turn about, and laugh at your own jest. }

 Or if your life be one continued treat,
If to live well means nothing but to eat;
Up, up! cries gluttony, 'tis break of day,
Go drive the deer, and drag the finny prey;
With hounds and horns go hunt an appetite--
So Russel did, but could not eat at night,
Called happy dog! the beggar at his door,
And envied thirst and hunger to the poor.

 Or shall we every decency confound,

Through taverns, stews, and bagnios take our round,
Go dine with Chartres, in each vice out-do
K---l's lewd cargo, or Ty---y's crew,
From Latian Syrens, French Circean feasts,
Return well travelled, and transformed to beasts.
  If, after all, we must with Wilmot own,
The cordial drop of life is love alone,
And Swift cry wisely, "Vive la Bagatelle!"
The man that loves and laughs, must sure do well.
Adieu--if this advice appear the worst,
E'en take the counsel which I gave you first:
Or better precepts if you can impart,
Why do, I'll follow them with all my heart.

THE FIRST EPISTLE OF THE SECOND BOOK OF HORACE.

ADVERTISEMENT.

The Reflections of Horace, and the Judgments past in his Epistle to Augustus, seemed so seasonable to the present Times, that I could not help applying them to the use of my own Country. The Author thought them considerable enough to address them to his Prince; whom he paints with all the great and good qualities of a Monarch, upon whom the Romans depended for the Increase of an Absolute Empire. But to make the Poem entirely English, I was willing to add one or two of those which contribute to the Happiness of a Free People, and are more consistent with the Welfare of our Neighbours.

This Epistle will show the learned World to have fallen into Two mistakes: one, that Augustus was a Patron of Poets in general; whereas he not only prohibited all but the Best Writers to name him, but recommended that Care even to the Civil Magistrate: Admonebat Praetores, ne paterentur Nomen suum obsolefieri, etc. The other, that this Piece was only a general Discourse of Poetry; whereas it was an Apology for the Poets, in order to render Augustus more their Patron. Horace here pleads the Cause of his Contemporaries, first against the Taste of the Town, whose humour it was to magnify the Authors of the preceding Age; secondly against the Court and Nobility, who encouraged only the Writers for the Theatre; and lastly against the Emperor himself, who had conceived them of little Use to the Government. He shows (by a View of the Progress of Learning, and the Change of Taste among the Romans) that the Introduction of the Polite Arts of Greece had given the Writers of his Time great advantages over their Predecessors; that their Morals were much improved, and the Licence of those ancient Poets restrained: that Satire and Comedy were become more just and useful; that, whatever extravagances were left on the Stage, were owing to the Ill Taste of the Nobility; that Poets, under due Regulations, were in many respects useful to the State, and concludes, that it was upon them the Emperor himself must depend for his Fame with Posterity.

We may farther learn from this Epistle, that Horace made his Court to this great Prince by writing with a decent Freedom toward him, with a just Contempt of his low Flatterers, and with a manly Regard to his own Character. P.

EPISTLE I. TO AUGUSTUS.

While you, great patron of mankind! sustain
The balanced world, and open all the main;
Your country, chief, in arms abroad defend,
At home, with morals, arts, and laws amend;
How shall the muse from such a monarch, steal
An hour, and not defraud the public weal?
  Edward and Henry, now the boast of fame,
And virtuous Alfred, a more sacred name,
After a life of generous toils endured,
The Gaul subdued, or property secured,
Ambition humbled, mighty cities stormed,
Our laws established, and the world reformed;
Closed their long glories with a sigh, to find
Th' unwilling gratitude of base mankind!
All human virtue, to its latest breath,
Finds envy never conquered but by death.
The great Alcides, every labour past,
Had still this monster to subdue at last.
Sure fate of all, beneath whose rising ray
Each star of meaner merit fades away!
Oppressed we feel the beam directly beat,
Those suns of glory please not till they set.
  To thee, the world its present homage pays,
The harvest early, but mature the praise:
Great friend of liberty! in kings a name
Above all Greek, above all Roman fame:
Whose word is truth, as sacred and revered,
As heaven's own oracles from altars heard.
Wonder of kings! like whom, to mortal eyes

None e'er has risen, and none e'er shall rise.
  Just in one instance be it yet confest
Your people, sir, are partial in the rest:
Foes to all living worth except your own,
And advocates for folly dead and gone.
Authors, like coins, grow dear as they grow old;
It is the rust we value, not the gold.
Chaucer's worst ribaldry is learned by rote,
And beastly Skelton heads of houses quote:
One likes no language but the Faery Queen;
A Scot will fight for Christ's Kirk o' the Green:
And each true Briton is to Ben so civil,
He swears the Muses met him at the devil.

  Though justly Greece her eldest sons admires,
Why should not we be wiser than our sires?
In every public virtue we excel;
We build, we paint, we sing, we dance as well,
And learned Athens to our art must stoop,
Could she behold us tumbling through a hoop.

  If time improve our wit as well as wine,
Say at what age a poet grows divine?
Shall we or shall we not account him so,
Who died, perhaps, a hundred years ago?
End all dispute; and fix the year precise
When British bards begin t' immortalise?

  "Who lasts a century can have no flaw,
I hold that wit a classic, good in law."

  Suppose he wants a year, will you compound;
And shall we deem him ancient, right and sound,
Or damn to all eternity at once,
At ninety-nine, a modern and a dunce?

  "We shall not quarrel for a year or two;
By courtesy of England, he may do."

Then by the rule that made the horse-tail bear,
I pluck out year by year, as hair by hair,
And melt down ancients like a heap of snow:
While you to measure merits, look in Stowe,
And estimating authors by the year
Bestow a garland only on a bier.
  Shakespeare (whom you and every play-house bill
Style the divine, the matchless, what you will)
For gain, not glory, winged his roving flight,
And grew immortal in his own despite.
Ben, old and poor, as little seemed to heed
The life to come, in every poet's creed.
Who now reads Cowley? if he pleases yet,
His moral pleases, not his pointed wit;
Forget his epic, nay Pindaric art;
But still I love the language of his heart.
  "Yet surely, surely, these were famous men!
What boy but hears the sayings of old Ben?
In all debates where Critics bears a part,
Not one but nods, and talks of Jonson's art,
Of Shakespeare's nature, and of Cowley's wit;
How Beaumont's judgment checked what Fletcher writ;
How Shadwell hasty, Wycherley was slow;
But for the passions, Southern sure and Rowe.
These, only these, support the crowded stage,
From eldest Heywood down to Cibber's age."
  All this may be; the people's voice is odd,
It is, and it is not, the voice of God.
To Gammer Gurton if it give the bays,
And yet deny the careless husband praise.
Or say our fathers never broke a rule;
Why then, I say, the public is a fool.
But let them own, that greater faults than we

They had, and greater virtues, I'll agree.
Spenser himself affects the obsolete,
And Sidney's verse halts ill on Roman feet:
Milton's strong pinion now not Heaven can bound,
Now serpent-like, in prose he sweeps the ground,
In quibbles angel and archangel join,
And God the Father turns a school divine.
Not that I'd lop the beauties from his book,
Like slashing Bentley with his desperate hook,
Or damn all Shakespeare, like the affected fool
At court, who hates whate'er he read at school.
  But for the wits of either Charles's days,
The mob of gentlemen who wrote with ease;
Sprat, Carew, Sedley, and a hundred more,
(Like twinkling stars the miscellanies o'er)
One simile, that solitary shines
In the dry desert of a thousand lines,
Or lengthened thought that gleams through many a page,
Has sanctified whole poems for an age.
I lose my patience, and I own it too,
When works are censured, not as bad but new;
While if our elders break all reason's laws,
These fools demand not pardon, but applause.
  On Avon's bank, where flowers eternal blow,
If I but ask, if any weed can grow;
One tragic sentence if I dare deride
Which Betterton's grave action dignified,
Or well-mouthed Booth with emphasis proclaims,
(Though but, perhaps, a muster-roll of names)
How will our fathers rise up in a rage,
And swear, all shame is lost in George's age!
You'd think no fools disgraced the former reign,
Did not some grave examples yet remain,

Who scorn a lad should teach his father skill,
And, having once been wrong, will be so still.
He, who to seem more deep than you or I,
Extols old bards, or Merlin's Prophecy,
Mistake him not; he envies, not admires,
And to debase the sons, exalts the sires.
Had ancient times conspired to disallow
What then was new, what had been ancient now?
Or what remained, so worthy to be read
By learned critics, of the mighty dead?
   In days of ease, when now the weary sword
Was sheathed, and luxury with Charles restored;
In every taste of foreign courts improved,
"All, by the king's example, lived and loved."
Then peers grew proud in horsemanship t' excel,
Newmarket's glory rose, as Britain's fell;
The soldier breathed the gallantries of France,
And every flowery courtier wrote romance.
Then marble, softened into life, grew warm:
And yielding metal flowed to human form:
Lely on animated canvas stole
The sleepy eye, that spoke the melting soul.
No wonder then, when all was love and sport,
The willing Muses were debauched at court:
On each enervate string they taught the note
To pant, or tremble through an eunuch's throat.
   But Britain, changeful as a child at play,
Now calls in princes, and now turns away.
Now Whig, now Tory, what we loved we hate;
Now all for pleasure, now for Church and State;
Now for prerogative, and now for laws;
Effects unhappy from a noble cause.
   Time was, a sober Englishman would knock

His servants up, and rise by five o'clock,
Instruct his family in every rule,
And send his wife to church, his son to school.
To worship like his fathers, was his care;
To teach their frugal virtues to his heir;
To prove, that luxury could never hold;
And place, on good security, his gold.
Now times are changed, and one poetic itch
Has seized the court and city, poor and rich:
Sons, sires, and grandsires, all will wear the bays,
Our wives read Milton, and our daughters plays,
To theatres, and to rehearsals throng,
And all our grace at table is a song.
I, who so oft renounce the Muses, lie,
Not ----'s self e'er tells more fibs than I;
When sick of Muse, our follies we deplore,
And promise our best friends to rhyme no more;
We wake next morning in a raging fit,
And call for pen and ink to show our wit.

  He served a 'prenticeship, who sets up shop;
Ward tried on puppies, and the poor, his drop;
Even Radcliff's doctors travel first to France,
Nor dare to practise till they've learned to dance.
Who builds a bridge that never drove a pile?
(Should Ripley venture, all the world would smile)
But those who cannot write, and those who can,
All rhyme, and scrawl, and scribble, to a man.

  Yet, sir, reflect, the mischief is not great;
These madmen never hurt the Church or State;
Sometimes the folly benefits mankind;
And rarely av'rice taints the tuneful mind.
Allow him but his plaything of a pen,
He ne'er rebels, or plots, like other men:

Flight of cashiers, or mobs, he'll never mind;
And knows no losses while the Muse is kind.
To cheat a friend, or ward, he leaves to Peter;
The good man heaps up nothing but mere metre,
Enjoys his garden and his book in quiet;
And then--a perfect hermit in his diet.
  Of little use the man you may suppose,
Who says in verse what others say in prose;
Yet let me show, a poet's of some weight,
And (though no soldier) useful to the State.
What will a child learn sooner than a song?
What better teach a foreigner the tongue?
What's long or short, each accent where to place,
And speak in public with some sort of grace?
I scarce can think him such a worthless thing,
Unless he praise some monster of a king;
Or virtue, or religion turn to sport,
To please a lewd or unbelieving court.
Unhappy Dryden!--In all Charles's days,
Roscommon only boasts unspotted bays;
And in our own (excuse some courtly stains)
No whiter page than Addison remains.
He, from the taste obscene reclaims our youth,
And sets the passions on the side of truth,
Forms the soft bosom with the gentlest art,
And pours each human virtue in the heart.
Let Ireland tell, how wit upheld her cause,
Her trade supported, and supplied her laws;
And leave on Swift this grateful verse engraved:
'The rights a court attacked, a poet saved.'
Behold the hand that wrought a nation's cure,
Stretched to relieve the idiot and the poor,
Proud vice to brand, or injured worth adorn,

And stretch the ray to ages yet unborn.
Not but there are, who merit other palms;
Hopkins and Sternhold glad the heart with psalms:
The boys and girls whom charity maintains,
Implore your help in these pathetic strains:
How could devotion touch the country pews,
Unless the gods bestowed a proper Muse?
Verse cheers their leisure, verse assists their work,
Verse prays for peace, or sings down Pope and Turk.
The silenced preacher yields to potent strain,
And feels that grace his prayer besought in vain;
The blessing thrills through all the lab'ring throng,
And Heaven is won by violence of song.
  Our rural ancestors, with little blest,
Patient of labour when the end was rest,
Indulged the day that housed their annual grain,
With feasts, and off'rings, and a thankful strain:
The joy their wives, their sons, and servants share,
Ease of their toil, and partners of their care:
The laugh, the jest, attendants on the bowl,
Smoothed every brow, and opened every soul:
With growing years the pleasing licence grew,
And taunts alternate innocently flew.
But times corrupt, and Nature, ill-inclined,
Produced the point that left a sting behind;
Till friend with friend, and families at strife,
Triumphant malice raged through private life.
Who felt the wrong, or feared it, took th' alarm,
Appealed to law, and justice lent her arm.
At length, by wholesome dread of statutes bound,
The poets learned to please, and not to wound:
Most warped to flatt'ry's side; but some more nice,
Preserved the freedom, and forebore the vice.

Hence satire rose, that just the medium hit,
And heals with morals what it hurts with wit.
  We conquered France, but felt our captive's charms;
Her arts victorious triumphed o'er our arms;
Britain to soft refinements less a foe,
Wit grew polite, and numbers learned to flow.
Waller was smooth; but Dryden taught to join }
The varying verse, the full-resounding line, }
The long majestic march, and energy divine. }
Though still some traces of our rustic vein
And splay-foot verse, remained, and will remain.
Late, very late, correctness grew our care,
When the tired nation breathed from civil war.
Exact Racine, and Corneille's noble fire,
Showed us that France had something to admire.
Not but the tragic spirit was our own,
And full in Shakespeare, fair in Otway shone:
But Otway failed to polish or refine,
And fluent Shakespeare scarce effaced a line.
E'en copious Dryden wanted, or forgot
The last and greatest art, the art to blot.
Some doubt, if equal pains, or equal fire
The humbler Muse of comedy require.
But in known images of life, I guess
The labour greater, as th' indulgence less.
Observe how seldom even the best succeed:
Tell me if Congreve's fools are fools indeed?
What pert, low dialogue has Farquhar writ!
How Van wants grace, who never wanted wit!
The stage how loosely does Astraea tread,
Who fairly puts all characters to bed!
And idle Cibber, how he breaks the laws,
To make poor Pinky eat with vast applause!

But fill their purse, our poet's work is done,
Alike to them, by pathos or by pun.
    O you! whom vanity's light bark conveys
On fame's mad voyage by the wind of praise,
With what a shifting gale your course you ply,
For ever sunk too low, or borne too high!
Who pants for glory finds but short repose,
A breath revives him, or a breath o'erthrows.
Farewell the stage! if just as thrives the play,
The silly bard grows fat, or falls away.
    There still remains, to mortify a wit,
The many-headed monster of the pit;
A senseless, worthless, and unhonoured crowd;
Who, to disturb their betters mighty proud,
Clatt'ring their sticks before ten lines are spoke,
Call for the farce, the bear, or the black-joke.
What dear delight to Britons farce affords!
Ever the taste of mobs, but now of lords;
(Taste, that eternal wanderer, which flies
From heads to ears, and now from ears to eyes).
The play stands still; damn action and discourse,
Back fly the scenes, and enter foot and horse;
Pageants on pageants, in long order drawn,
Peers, Heralds, Bishops, ermine, gold, and lawn;
The champion too! and, to complete the jest,
Old Edward's armour beams on Cibber's breast,
With laughter sure Democritus had died,
Had he beheld an audience gape so wide.
Let bear or elephant be e'er so white,
The people, sure, the people are the sight!
Ah luckless poet! stretch thy lungs and roar,
That bear or elephant shall heed thee more;
While all its throats the gallery extends,

And all the thunder of the pit ascends!
Loud as the wolves, on Orcas' stormy steep,
Howl to the roarings of the Northern deep,
Such is the shout, the long-applauding note,
At Quin's high plume, or Oldfield's petticoat;
Or when from court a birthday suit bestowed,
Sinks the lost actor in the tawdry load.
Booth enters--hark! the universal peal!
"But has he spoken?" Not a syllable.
What shook the stage, and made the people stare?
Cato's long wig, flowered gown, and lacquered chair.
  Yet lest you think I rally more than teach,
Or praise malignly arts I cannot reach,
Let me for once presume t' instruct the times,
To know the poet from the man of rhymes:
'Tis he, who gives my breast a thousand pains,
Can make me feel each passion that he feigns;
Enrage, compose, with more than magic art,
With pity, and with terror, tear my heart;
And snatch me, o'er the earth, or through the air,
To Thebes, to Athens, when he will, and where.
  But not this part of the poetic state
Alone, deserves the favour of the great;
Think of those authors, sir, who would rely
More on a reader's sense, than gazer's eye.
Or who shall wander where the Muses sing?
Who climb their mountain, or who taste their spring?
How shall we fill a library with wit,
When Merlin's cave is half unfurnished yet?
  My liege! why writers little claim your thought,
I guess; and, with their leave, will tell the fault:
We poets are (upon a poet's word)
Of all mankind, the creatures most absurd:

The season, when to come, and when to go,
To sing, or cease to sing, we never know;
And if we will recite nine hours in ten,
You lose your patience, just like other men.
Then too we hurt ourselves, when to defend
A single verse, we quarrel with a friend;
Repeat unasked; lament, the wit's too fine
For vulgar eyes, and point out every line.
But most, when straining with too weak a wing,
We needs will write epistles to the King;
And from the moment we oblige the town,
Expect a place, or pension from the Crown;
Or dubbed historians, by express command,
T' enrol your triumphs o'er the seas and land,
Be called to Court to plan some work divine,
As once for Louis, Boileau and Racine.
   Yet think, great sir! (so many virtues shown)
Ah think, what poet best may make them known?
Or choose at least some minister of grace,
Fit to bestow the laureate's weighty place.
   Charles, to late times to be transmitted fair,
Assigned his figure to Bernini's care;
And great Nassau to Kneller's hand decreed
To fix him graceful on the bounding steed;
So well in paint and stone they judged of merit:
But kings in wit may want discerning spirit.
The hero William and the martyr Charles,
One knighted Blackmore, and one pensioned Quarles;
Which made old Ben, and surly Dennis swear,
"No Lord's anointed, but a Russian bear."
   Not with such majesty, such bold relief,
The forms august, of king, or conquering chief,
E'er swelled on marble; as in verse have shined

(In polished verse) the manners and the mind.
Oh! could I mount on the Maeonian wing,
Your arms, your actions, your repose to sing!
What seas you traversed, and what fields you fought!
Your country's peace, how oft, how dearly bought!
How barb'rous rage subsided at your word,
And nations wondered while they dropped the sword!
How, when you nodded, o'er the land and deep,
Peace stole her wing, and wrapped the world in sleep;
Till earth's extremes your mediation own,
And Asia's tyrants tremble at your throne--
But verse, alas! your majesty disdains;
And I'm not used to panegyric strains:
The zeal of fools offends at any time,
But most of all, the zeal of fools in rhyme.
Besides, a fate attends on all I write,
That when I aim at praise, they say I bite.
A vile encomium doubly ridicules:
There's nothing blackens like the ink of fools.
If true, a woeful likeness; and if lies,
"Praise undeserved is scandal in disguise:"
Well may he blush, who gives it, or receives;
And when I flatter, let my dirty leaves
(Like journals, odes, and such forgotten things
As Eusden, Philips, Settle, writ of kings)
Clothe spice, line trunks, or, flutt'ring in a row,
Befringe the rails of Bedlam and Soho.

THE SECOND EPISTLE OF THE SECOND BOOK OF HORACE.

"Ludentis speciem dabit, et torquebitur." HOR. (v.124.)

Dear Colonel, Cobham's and your country's friend!
You love a verse, take such as I can send.
A Frenchman comes, presents you with his boy,
Bows and begins--"This lad, sir, is of Blois:
Observe his shape how clean! his locks how curled!
My only son, I'd have him see the world:
His French is pure; his voice too--you shall hear.
Sir, he's your slave for twenty pound a year.
Mere wax as yet, you fashion him with ease,
Your barber, cook, upholsterer, what you please:
A perfect genius at an opera song--
To say too much might do my honour wrong.
Take him with all his virtues, on my word;
His whole ambition was to serve a lord:
But, sir, to you, with what would I not part?
Though faith, I fear 'twill break his mother's heart.
Once (and but once) I caught him in a lie,
And then, unwhipped, he had the grace to cry:
The fault he has I fairly shall reveal,
(Could you o'erlook but that) it is to steal."
   If, after this, you took the graceless lad,
Could you complain, my friend, he proved so bad?
Faith, in such case, if you should prosecute,
I think Sir Godfrey should decide the suit:
Who sent the thief that stole the cash away,

And punished him that put it in his way.
   Consider then, and judge me in this light;
I told you when I went, I could not write;
You said the same; and are you discontent
With laws to which you gave your own assent?
Nay worse, to ask for verse at such a time!
D'ye think me good for nothing but to rhyme?
   In Anna's wars, a soldier poor and old
Had dearly earned a little purse of gold;
Tired with a tedious march, one luckless night,
He slept, poor dog! and lost it to a doit.
This put the man in such a desperate mind, }
Between revenge, and grief, and hunger joined }
Against the foe, himself, and all mankind, }
He leaped the trenches, scaled a castle wall,
Tore down a standard, took the fort and all.
"Prodigious well," his great commander cried,
Gave him much praise and some reward beside.
Next pleased his excellence a town to batter:
(Its name I know not, and it's no great matter).
"Go on, my friend," he cried, "see yonder walls,
Advance and conquer! go where glory calls!
More honours, more rewards attend the brave."
Don't you remember what reply he gave?
"D'ye think me, noble general, such a sot?
Let him take castles who has ne'er a groat."
   Bred up at home, full early I begun
To read in Greek the wrath of Peleus' son.
Besides, my father taught me from a lad,
The better art to know the good from bad:
(And little sure imported to remove,
To hunt for truth in Maudlin's learned grove).
But knottier points we knew not half so well,

Deprived us soon of our paternal cell;
And certain laws, by sufferers thought unjust,
Denied all posts of profit or of trust:
Hopes after hopes of pious Papists failed,
While mighty William's thundering arm prevailed,
For right hereditary taxed and fined,
He stuck to poverty with peace of mind;
And me, the Muses helped to undergo it;
Convict a Papist he, and I a poet.
But (thanks to Homer) since I live and thrive,
Indebted to no prince or peer alive,
Sure I should want the care of ten Monroes,
If I would scribble rather than repose.
Years following years, steal something every day,
At last they steal us from ourselves away;
In one our frolics, one amusements end,
In one a mistress drops, in one a friend:
This subtle thief of life, this paltry time,
What will it leave me, if it snatch my rhyme?
If every wheel of that unwearied mill,
That turned ten thousand verses, now stands still?
　　But after all, what would you have me do?
When out of twenty I can please not two;
When this heroics only deigns to praise,
Sharp satire that, and that Pindaric lays?
One likes the pheasant's wing, and one the leg;
The vulgar boil, the learned roast an egg;
Hard task! to hit the palate of such guests,
When Oldfield loves what Dartineuf detests.
　　But grant I may relapse, for want of grace,
Again to rhyme, can London be the place?
Who there his Muse, or self, or soul attends,
In crowds, and courts, law, business, feasts, and friends?

My counsel sends to execute a deed;
A poet begs me I will hear him read;
'In Palace Yard at nine you'll find me there--'
'At ten for certain, sir, in Bloomsbury Square--'
'Before the Lords at twelve my cause comes on--'
'There's a rehearsal, sir, exact at one.--'
"Oh, but a wit can study in the streets,
And raise his mind above the mob he meets."
Not quite so well, however, as one ought;
A hackney coach may chance to spoil a thought;
And then a nodding beam or pig of lead,
God knows, may hurt the very ablest head.
Have you not seen, at Guildhall's narrow pass,
Two aldermen dispute it with an ass?
And peers give way, exalted as they are,
Even to their own s-r-v-ance in a car?
　Go, lofty poet! and in such a crowd,
Sing thy sonorous verse--but not aloud.
Alas! to grottoes and to groves we run,
To ease and silence, every Muse's son:
Blackmore himself, for any grand effort,
Would drink and doze at Tooting or Earl's Court.
How shall I rhyme in this eternal roar?
How match the bards whom none e'er matched before?
The man, who, stretched in Isis' calm retreat,
To books and study gives seven years complete,
See! strewed with learned dust, his night-cap on,
He walks, an object new beneath the sun!
The boys flock round him, and the people stare: }
So stiff, so mute! some statue you would swear, }
Stepped from its pedestal to take the air! }
And here, while town, and court, and city roars,
With mobs, and duns, and soldiers at their doors;

Shall I, in London, act this idle part?
Composing songs for fools to get by heart?
The Temple late two brother sergeants saw,
Who deemed each other oracles of law;
With equal talents these congenial souls,
One lulled th' Exchequer, and one stunned the Rolls;
Each had a gravity would make you split,
And shook his head at Murray as a wit.
"'Twas, sir, your law"--and "Sir, your eloquence--"
"Yours, Cowper's manner"--and "yours, Talbot's sense."
Thus we dispose of all poetic merit,
Yours Milton's genius, and mine Homer's spirit.
Call Tibbald Shakespeare, and he'll swear the nine,
Dear Cibber! never matched one ode of thine.
Lord! how we strut through Merlin's cave, to see
No poets there, but Stephen, you, and me.
Walk with respect behind, while we at ease
Weave laurel crowns, and take what names we please.
"My dear Tibullus!" if that will not do,
"Let me be Horace, and be Ovid you:
Or, I'm content, allow me Dryden's strains,
And you shall rise up Otway for your pains."
Much do I suffer, much, to keep in peace
This jealous, waspish, wrong-head, rhyming race;
And much must flatter, if the whim should bite
To court applause by printing what I write:
But let the fit pass o'er, I'm wise enough,
To stop my ears to their confounded stuff.
    In vain bad rhymers all mankind reject,
They treat themselves with most profound respect;
'Tis to small purpose that you hold your tongue:
Each praised within, is happy all day long;
But how severely with themselves proceed

The men, who write such verse as we can read?
Their own strict judges, not a word they spare
That wants, or force, or light, or weight, or care,
Howe'er unwillingly it quits its place,
Nay though at Court, perhaps, it may find grace:
Such they'll degrade; and sometimes, in its stead,
In downright charity revive the dead;
Mark where a bold expressive phrase appears,
Bright through the rubbish of some hundred years;
Command old words that long have slept, to wake,
Words that wise Bacon or brave Raleigh spake;
Or bid the new be English, ages hence,
(For use will farther what's begot by sense)
Pour the full tide of eloquence along, }
Serenely pure, and yet divinely strong, }
Rich with the treasures of each foreign tongue; }
Prune the luxuriant, the uncouth refine,
But show no mercy to an empty line:
Then polish all, with so much life and ease,
You think 'tis nature, and a knack to please:
"But ease in writing flows from art, not chance;
As those move easiest who have learned to dance."
  If such the plague and pains to write by rule,
Better, say I, be pleased and play the fool;
Call, if you will, bad rhyming a disease,
It gives men happiness, or leaves them ease.
There lived in primo Georgii, they record,
A worthy member, no small fool, a lord;
Who, though the House was up, delighted sate,
Heard, noted, answered, as in full debate:
In all but this, a man of sober life,
Fond of his friend, and civil to his wife;
Not quite a madman, though a pasty fell,

And much too wise to walk into a well.
Him, the damned doctors and his friends immured,
They bled, they cupped, they purged; in short, they cured.
Whereat the gentleman began to stare--
"My friends!" he cried, "plague take you for your care!
That from a patriot of distinguished note,
Have bled and purged me to a simple vote."
Well, on the whole, plain prose must be my fate:
Wisdom (curse on it) will come soon or late.
There is a time when poets will grow dull:
I'll e'en leave verses to the boys at school:
To rules of poetry no more confined,
I learn to smooth and harmonise my mind,
Teach every thought within its bounds to roll,
And keep the equal measure of the soul.

   Soon as I enter at my country door
My mind resumes the thread it dropt before;
Thoughts, which at Hyde Park Corner I forgot,
Meet and rejoin me, in the pensive grot.
There all alone, and compliments apart,
I ask these sober questions of my heart.

   If, when the more you drink, the more you crave,
You tell the doctor; when the more you have,
The more you want; why not with equal ease
Confess as well your folly, as disease?
The heart resolves this matter in a thrice,
"Men only feel the smart but not the vice."

   When golden angels cease to cure the evil,
You give all royal witchcraft to the devil;
When servile chaplains cry, that birth and place
Endure a peer with honour, truth, and grace,
Look in that breast, most dirty D----! be fair,
Say, can you find out one such lodger there?

Yet still, not heeding what your heart can teach,
You go to church to hear these flatterers preach.
   Indeed, could wealth bestow or wit or merit,
A grain of courage, or a spark of spirit,
The wisest man might blush, I must agree,
If D*** loved sixpence more than he.
   If there be truth in law, and use can give
A property, that's yours on which you life.
Delightful Abs Court, if its fields afford
Their fruits to you, confesses you its lord;
All Worldly's hens, nay partridge, sold to town:
His venison too, a guinea makes your own:
He bought at thousands, what with better wit
You purchase as you want, and bit by bit;
Now, or long since, what difference will be found?
You pay a penny, and he paid a pound.
   Heathcote himself, and such large-acred men,
Lords of fat E'sham, or of Lincoln fen,
Buy every stick of wood that lends them heat,
Buy every pullet they afford to eat.
Yet these are wights, who fondly call their own
Half that the Devil o'erlooks from Lincoln town.
The laws of God, as well as of the land,
Abhor, a perpetuity should stand:
Estates have wings and hang in fortune's power
Loose on the point of every wavering hour,
Ready, by force, or of your own accord,
By sale, at least by death, to change their lord.
Man? and for ever? wretch! what wouldst thou have?
Heir urges heir, like wave impelling wave.
All vast possessions (just the same the case
Whether you call them villa, park, or chase).
Alas, my Bathurst! what will they avail?

Join Cotswold hills to Saperton's fair dale,
Let rising granaries and temples here,
There mingled farms and pyramids appear,
Link towns to towns with avenues of oak,
Enclose whole downs in walls, 'tis all a joke!
Inexorable death shall level all,
And trees, and stones, and farms, and farmer fall.
    Gold, silver, ivory, vases sculptured high,
Paint, marble, gems, and robes of Persian dye,
There are who have not--and thank heaven there are,
Who, if they have not, think not worth their care,
Talk what you will of taste, my friend, you'll find,
Two of a face, as soon as of a mind.
Why, of two brothers, rich and restless one
Ploughs, burns, manures, and toils from sun to sun;
The other slights, for women, sports, and wines,
All Townshend's turnips, and all Grosvenor's mines;
Why one like Bu--with pay and scorn content,
Bows and votes on, in Court and Parliament;
One, driven by strong benevolence of soul,
Shall fly, like Oglethorpe, from pole to pole;
Is known alone to that directing power,
Who forms the genius in the natal hour;
That God of Nature, who, within us still,
Inclines our action, not constrains our will:
Various of temper, as of face or frame.
Each individual: His great end the same.
    Yes, sir, how small soever be my heap,
A part I will enjoy, as well as keep.
My heir may sigh, and think it want of grace
A man so poor would live without a place;
But sure no statute in his favour says
How free, or frugal, I shall pass my days:

I, who at some times spend, at others spare,
Divided between carelessness and care.
'Tis one thing madly to disperse my store;
Another, not to heed to treasure more!
Glad, like a boy, to snatch the first good day,
And pleased, if sordid want be far away.

What is't to me (a passenger, God wot)
Whether my vessel be first-rate or not?
The ship itself may make a better figure,
But I that sail, am neither less nor bigger,
I neither strut with every favouring breath,
Nor strive with all the tempest in my teeth.
In power, wit, figure, virtue, fortune, placed
Behind the foremost and before the last.

"But why all this of avarice? I have none."
I wish you joy, sir, of a tyrant gone;
But does no other lord it at this hour,
As wild and mad: the avarice of power?
Does neither rage inflame, nor fear appal?
Not the black fear of death, that saddens all?
With terrors round, can Reason hold her throne,
Despise the known, nor tremble at the unknown?
Survey both worlds, intrepid and entire,
In spite of witches, devils, dreams, and fire?
Pleased to look forward, pleased to look behind,
And count each birthday with a grateful mind?
Has life no sourness, drawn so near its end?
Canst thou endure a foe, forgive a friend?
Has age but melted the rough parts away,
As winter fruits grow mild ere they decay?
Or will you think, my friend, your business done,
When, of a hundred thorns, you pull out one?

Learn to live well, or fairly make your will;

You've played, and loved, and ate, and drank your fill:
Walk sober off; before a sprightlier age
Comes tittering on, and shoves you from the stage;
Leave such to trifle with more grace and ease,
Where folly pleases, and whose follies please.

THE SATIRES OF DR. JOHN DONNE, DEAN OF ST. PAUL'S. VERSIFIED.

"Quid vetat et nosmet *Lucili* scripta legentes
Quaerere, num illius, num rerum dura negarit
Versiculos natura magis factos, et euntes
Mollius?"

HOR. (Sat. LX. 56-9).

SATIRE II.

Yes; thank my stars! as early as I knew
This town, I had the sense to hate it too;
Yet here; as even in hell, there must be still
One giant-vice, so excellently ill,
That all beside, one pities, not abhors;
As who knows Sappho, smiles at other whores.
  I grant that poetry's a crying sin;
It brought (no doubt) the excise and army in:

Catched like the plague, or love, the Lord knows how,
But that the cure is starving, all allow.
Yet like the Papist's, is the poet's state,
Poor and disarmed, and hardly worth your hate!
Here a lean bard, whose wit could never give
Himself a dinner, makes an actor live:
The thief condemned, in law already dead,
So prompts, and saves a rogue who cannot read.
Thus, as the pipes of some carved organ move,
The gilded puppets dance and mount above.
Heaved by the breath the inspiring bellows blow:
The inspiring bellows lie and pant below.

One sings the fair; but songs no longer move;
No rat is rhymed to death, nor maid to love:
In love's, in nature's spite, the siege they hold,
And scorn the flesh, the devil, and all but gold.

These write to lords, some mean reward to get,
As needy beggars sing at doors for meat.
Those write because all write, and so have still
Excuse for writing, and for writing ill.

Wretched, indeed! but far more wretched yet
Is he who makes his meal on others' wit:
'Tis changed, no doubt, from what it was before;
His rank digestion makes it wit no more:
Sense, past through him, no longer is the same;
For food digested takes another name.

I pass o'er all those confessors and martyrs
Who live like S-tt-n, or who die like Chartres,
Out-cant old Esdras, or out-drink his heir,
Out-usure Jews, or Irishmen out-swear;
Wicked as pages, who in early years
Act sins which Prisca's confessor scarce hears.
Even those I pardon, for whose sinful sake

Schoolmen new tenements in hell must make;
Of whose strange crimes no canonist can tell
In what Commandment's large contents they dwell.
    One, one man only breeds my just offence;
Whom crimes gave wealth, and wealth gave impudence:
Time brings all natural events to pass,
And made him an attorney of an ass.
No young divine, new beneficed, can be
More pert, more proud, more positive than he.
What further could I wish the fop to do,
But turn a wit, and scribble verses too;
Pierce the soft labyrinth of a lady's ear
With rhymes of this per cent. and that per year?
Or court a wife, spread out his wily parts,
Like nets or lime-twigs, for rich widows' hearts;
Call himself barrister to every wench,
And woo in language of the pleas and bench?
Language, which Boreas might to Auster hold
More rough than forty Germans when they scold.
    Cursed be the wretch, so venal and so vain:
Paltry and proud, as drabs in Drury Lane.
'Tis such a bounty as was never known,
If Peter deigns to help you to your own:
What thanks, what praise, if Peter but supplies,
And what a solemn face if he denies!
Grave, as when prisoners shake the head and swear
'Twas only suretyship that brought 'em there.
His office keeps your parchment fates entire,
He starves with cold to save them from the fire;
For you he walks the streets through rain or dust,
For not in chariots Peter puts his trust;
For you he sweats and labours at the laws,
Takes God to witness he affects your cause,

And lies to every lord in every thing,
Like a king's favourite--or like a king.
These are the talents that adorn them all,
From wicked waters even to godly * *
Not more of simony beneath black gowns,
Nor more of bastardy in heirs to crowns.
In shillings and in pence at first they deal;
And steal so little, few perceive they steal;
Till, like the sea, they compass all the land,
From Scots to Wight, from mount to Dover strand:
And when rank widows purchase luscious nights,
Or when a duke to Jansen punts at White's,
Or City-heir in mortgage melts away;
Satan himself feels far less joy than they.
Piecemeal they win this acre first, then that,
Glean on, and gather up the whole estate.
Then strongly fencing ill-got wealth by law,
Indentures, covenants, articles thy draw,
Large as the fields themselves, and larger far
Than civil codes, with all their glosses, are;
So vast, our new divines, we must confess,
Are fathers of the Church for writing less.
But let them write for you, each rogue impairs
The deeds, and dexterously omits, ses heires;
No commentator can more slily pass
O'er a learned, unintelligible place;
Or, in quotation, shrewd divines leave out
Those words, that would against them clear the doubt.
　So Luther thought the Paternoster long,
When doomed to say his beads and even-song;
But having cast his cowl, and left those laws,
Adds to Christ's prayer, the Power and Glory clause.
　The lands are bought; but where are to be found

Those ancient woods, that shaded all the ground?
We see no new-built palaces aspire,
No kitchens emulate the vestal fire.
Where are those troops of poor, that thronged of yore
The good old landlord's hospitable door?
Well, I could wish, that still in lordly domes
Some beasts were killed, though not whole hecatombs;
That both extremes were banished from their walls,
Carthusian fasts, and fulsome bacchanals;
And all mankind might that just mean observe,
In which none e'er could surfeit, none could starve.
These as good works, 'tis true, we all allow;
But oh! these works are not in fashion now:
Like rich old wardrobes, things extremely rare,
Extremely fine, but what no man will wear.
    Thus much I've said, I trust, without offence;
Let no Court sycophant pervert my sense,
Nor sly informer watch these words to draw
Within the reach of treason, or the law.

SATIRE IV.

Well, if it be my time to quit the stage,
Adieu to all the follies of the age!
I die in charity with fool and knave,
Secure of peace at least beyond the grave.
I've had my purgatory here betimes,
And paid for all my satires, all my rhymes.
The poet's hell, its tortures, fiends, and flames,
To this were trifles, toys, and empty names.
    With foolish pride my heart was never fired,

Nor the vain itch to admire, or be admired;
I hoped for no commission from his Grace;
I bought no benefice, I begged no place;
Had no new verses, nor new suit to show;
Yet went to Court!--the Devil would have it so.
But, as the fool that in reforming days
Would go to Mass in jest (as story says)
Could not but think, to pay his fine was odd,
Since 'twas no formed design of serving God;
So was I punished, as if full as proud
As prone to ill, as negligent of good,
As deep in debt, without a thought to pay, }
As vain, as idle, and as false, as they }
Who live at Court, for going once that way! }
Scarce was I entered, when, behold! there came
A thing which Adam had been posed to name;
Noah had refused it lodging in his Ark,
Where all the race of reptiles might embark:
A verier monster, that on Afric's shore
The sun e'er got, or slimy Nilus bore,
Or Sloane or Woodward's wondrous shelves contain,
Nay, all that lying travellers can feign.
The watch would hardly let him pass at noon,
At night, would swear him dropped out of the moon.
One whom the mob, when next we find or make
A Popish plot, shall for a Jesuit take,
And the wise Justice starting from his chair
Cry: "By your priesthood tell me what you are?"
    Such was the wight; the apparel on his back
Though coarse, was reverend, and though bare, was black:
The suit, if by the fashion one might guess,
Was velvet in the youth of good Queen Bess,
But mere tuff-taffety what now remained;

So time, that changes all things, had ordained!
Our sons shall see it leisurely decay,
First turn plain rash, then vanish quite away.
   This thing has travelled, speaks each language too,
And know what's fit for very state to do;
Of whose best phrase and courtly accent joined,
He forms one tongue, exotic and refined,
Talkers I've learned to bear; Motteux I knew,
Henley himself I've heard, and Budgel too.
The doctor's wormwood style, the hash of tongues
A pedant makes, the storm of Gonson's lungs,
The whole artillery of the terms of war,
And (all those plagues in one) the bawling bar:
These I could bear; but not a rogue so civil,
Whose tongue will compliment you to the devil.
A tongue that can cheat widows, cancel scores,
Make Scots speak treason, cozen subtlest w***es,
With royal favourites in flattery vie,
And Oldmixon and Burnet both outlie.
   He spies me out, I whisper: "Gracious God!
What sin of mine could merit such a rod?
That all the shot of dulness now must be
From this thy blunderbuss discharged on me!"
"Permit" (he cries) "no stranger to your fame
To crave your sentiment, if ----'s your name.
What speech esteem you most?" "The King's," said I
"But the best words?"--"O, sir, the dictionary."
"You miss my aim; I mean the most acute
And perfect speaker?"--"Onslow, past dispute."
"But, sir, of writers?" "Swift, for closer style,
But Ho**y for a period of a mile."
"Why, yes, 'tis granted, these indeed may pass:
Good common linguists, and so Panurge was;

Nay troth the Apostles (though perhaps too rough)
Had once a pretty gift of tongues enough:
Yet these were all poor gentlemen! I dare
Affirm, 'twas travel made them what they were."
　Thus others' talents having nicely shown,
He came by sure transition to his own:
Till I cried out: "You prove yourself so able,
Pity! you was not Druggerman at Babel;
For had they found a linguist half so good
I make no question but the tower had stood."
"Obliging sir! for courts you sure were made:
Why then for ever buried in the shade?
Spirits like you should see and should be seen,
The King would smile on you--at least the Queen."
"Ah, gentle sir! you courtiers so cajole us--
But Tully has it, Nunquam minus solus:
And as for courts, forgive me, if I say
No lessons now are taught the Spartan way:
Though in his pictures lust be full displayed,
Few are the converts Aretine has made;
And though the Court show vice exceeding clear,
None should, by my advice, learn virtue there."
　At this entranced, he lifts his hands and eyes,
Squeaks like a high-stretched lutestring, and replies:
"Oh, 'tis the sweetest of all earthly things
To gaze on princes, and to talk of kings!"
"Then, happy man who shows the tombs!" said I,
"He dwells amidst the Royal Family;
He every day, from king to king can walk,
Of all our Harries, all our Edwards talk,
And get by speaking truth of monarchs dead,
What few can of the living, ease and bread."
"Lord, sir, a mere mechanic! strangely low,

And coarse of phrase--your English all are so.
How elegant your Frenchmen?" "Mine, d'ye mean?
I have but one, I hope the fellow's clean."
"Oh! sir, politely so! nay, let me die,
Your only wearing is your Paduasoy."
"Not, sir, my only, I have better still,
And this you see is but my dishabille--."
Wild to get loose, his patience I provoke,
Mistake, confound, object at all he spoke.
But as coarse iron, sharpened, mangles more,
And itch most hurts when angered to a sore;
So when you plague a fool, 'tis still the curse,
You only make the matter worse and worse.
   He past it o'er; affects an easy smile
At all my peevishness, and turns his style.
He asks, "What news?" I tell him of new plays,
New eunuchs, harlequins, and operas.
He hears, and as a still with simples in it
Between each drop it gives, stays half a minute,
Loth to enrich me with too quick replies,
By little and by little drops his lies.
Mere household trash! of birth-nights, balls, and shows,
More than ten Holinsheds, or Halls, or Stowes.
When the Queen frowned, or smiled, he knows; and what
A subtle minister may make of that;
Who sins with whom: who got his pension rug,
Or quickened a reversion by a drug;
Whose place is quartered out, three parts in four,
And whether to a bishop, or a w***e;
Who having lost his credit, pawned his rent,
Is therefore fit to have a Government;
Who in the secret, deals in stocks secure,
And cheats the unknowing widow and the poor;

Who makes a trust or charity a job,
And gets an Act of Parliament to rob;
Why turnpikes rise, and now no cit nor clown
Can gratis see the country, or the town;
Shortly no lad shall chuck, or lady vole,
But some excising courtier will have toll.
He tells what strumpet places sells for life,
What 'squire his lands, what citizen his wife:
And last (which proves him wiser still than all)
What lady's face is not a whited wall.
  As one of Woodward's patients, sick, and sore,
I puke, I nauseate--yet he thrusts in more:
Trims Europe's balance, tops the statesman's part,
And talks gazettes and post-boys o'er by heart.
Like a big wife at sight of loathsome meat
Ready to cast, I yawn, I sigh and sweat.
Then as a licensed spy, whom nothing can
Silence or hurt, he libels the great man;
Swears every place entailed for years to come,
In sure succession to the day of doom;
He names the price for every office paid,
And says our wars thrive ill, because delayed;
Nay hints, 'tis by connivance of the Court,
That Spain robs on, and Dunkirk's still a port.
Not more amazement seized on Circe's guests,
To see themselves fall endlong into beasts,
Than mine, to find a subject staid and wise
Already half turned traitor by surprise.
I felt the infection slide from him to me,
As in the ---- some give it to get free;
And quick to swallow me, methought I saw
One of our giant statutes ope its jaw.
  In that nice moment, as another lie

Stood just a-tilt, the minister came by.
To him he flies, and bows, and bows again,
Then, close as Umbra, joins the dirty train.
Not Fannius' self more impudently near,
When half his nose is in his Prince's ear.
I quaked at heart; and still afraid, to see
All the Court filled with stranger things than he,
Ran out as fast as one that pays his bail
And dreads more actions, hurries from a jail.
   Bear me, some god! oh, quickly bear me hence
To wholesome solitude, the nurse of sense:
Where Contemplation plumes her ruffled wings,
And the free soul looks down to pity kings!
There sober thought pursued the amusing theme,
Till fancy coloured it, and formed a dream.
A vision hermits can to hell transport,
And forced even me to see the damned at Court.
Not Dante dreaming all the infernal state,
Beheld such scenes of envy, sin, and hate.
Base fear becomes the guilty, not the free;
Suits tyrants, plunderers, but suits not me:
Shall I, the terror of this sinful town,
Care, if a liveried lord or smile or frown?
Who cannot flatter, and detest who can,
Tremble before a noble serving-man?
O, my fair mistress, Truth! shall I quit thee
For huffing, braggart, puffed nobility?
Thou, who since yesterday hast rolled o'er all
The busy, idle blockheads of the ball,
Hast thou, oh, sun! beheld an emptier fort,
Than such who swell this bladder of a Court?
Now plague on those who show a Court in wax!
It ought to bring all courtiers on their backs:

Such painted puppets! such a varnished race
Of hollow gewgaws, only dress and face!
Such waxen noses, stately staring things--
No wonder some folks bow, and think them kings.
  See! where the British youth, engaged no more
At Fig's, at White's, with felons, or a bore,
Pay their last duty to the Court and come
All fresh and fragrant, to the drawing-room;
In hues as gay, and odours as divine,
As the fair fields they sold to look so fine.
"That's velvet for a king!" the flatterer swears
'Tis true, for ten days hence 'twill be King Lear's.
Our Court may justly to our stage give rules,
That helps it both to fools-coats and to fools.
And why not players strut in courtiers' clothes?
For these are actors too, as well as those:
Wants reach all states; they beg but better drest,
And all is splended poverty at best.
Painted for sight, and essenced for the smell,
Like frigates fraught with spice and cochinel,
Sail in the ladies: how each pirate eyes
So weak a vessel, and so rich a prize!
Top-gallant he, and she in all her trim,
He boarding her, she striking sail to him:
"Dear Countess! you have charms all hearts to hit!"
And "Sweet Sir Fopling! you have so much wit!"
Such wits and beauties are not praised for nought,
For both the beauty and the wit are bought.
'Twould burst even Heraclitus with the spleen
To see those antics, Fopling and Courtin:
The presence seems, with things so richly odd,
The mosque of Mahound, or some queer Pagod.
See them survey their limbs by Durer's rules,

Of all beau-kind the best proportioned fools!
Adjust their clothes, and to confession draw
Those venial sins, an atom, or a straw;
But oh! what terrors must distract the soul
Convicted of that mortal crime, a hole;
Or should one pound of powder less bespread
Those monkey tails that wag behind their head.
Thus finished, and corrected to a hair,
They march, to prate their hour before the fair.
So first to preach a white-gloved chaplain goes,
With band of lily, and with cheek of rose,
Sweeter than Sharon, in immaculate trim,
Neatness itself impertinent in him.
Let but the ladies smile, and they are blest:
Prodigious! how the things protest, protest:
Peace, fools, or Gonson will for Papists seize you,
If once he catch you at your Jesu! Jesu!
  Nature made every fop to plague his brother,
Just as one beauty mortifies another.
But here's the captain that will plague them both,
Whose air cries Arm! whose very look's an oath:
The captain's honest, Sirs, and that's enough,
Though his soul's bullet, and his body buff.
He spits fore-right; his haughty chest before,
Like battering rams, beats open every door:
And with a face as red, and as awry,
As Herod's hangdogs in old tapestry,
Scarecrow to boys, the breeding woman's curse,
Has yet a strange ambition to look worse;
Confounds the civil, keeps the rude in awe,
Jests like a licensed fool, commands like law.
  Frighted, I quit the room, but leave it so
As men from jails to execution go;

For hung with deadly sins I see the wall,
And lined with giants deadlier than 'em all:
Each man an Askapart, of strength to toss
For quoits, both Temple Bar and Charing Cross.
Scared at the grizzly forms, I sweat, I fly,
And shake all o'er, like a discovered spy.

   Courts are too much for wits so weak as mine:
Charge them with Heaven's artillery, bold divine!
From such alone the great rebukes endure
Whose satire's sacred, and whose rage secure:

   'Tis mine to wash a few light stains, but theirs
To deluge sin, and drown a Court in tears.
However, what's now Apocrypha, my wit,
In time to come, may pass for holy writ.

EPILOGUE TO THE SATIRES.
IN TWO DIALOGUES.
WRITTEN IN MDCCXXXVIII.

DIALOGUE I.

   Fr. Not twice a twelvemonth you appear in print,
And when it comes, the Court see nothing in't.
You grow correct, that once with rapture writ,
And are, besides, too moral for a wit.
Decay of parts, alas! we all must feel--
Why now, this moment, don't I see you steal?
'Tis all from Horace; Horace long before ye

Said, "Tories called him Whig, and Whigs a Tory;"
And taught his Romans, in much better metre,
"To laugh at fools who put their trust in Peter."
   But Horace, sir, was delicate, was nice;
Bubo observes, he lashed no sort of vice;
Horace would say, Sir Billy served the crown,
Blunt could do business, H-ggins knew the town;
In Sappho touch the failings of the sex,
In reverend bishops note some small neglects,
And own, the Spaniard did a waggish thing,
Who cropped our ears, and sent them to the king.
His sly, polite, insinuating style
Could please at Court, and make Augustus smile:
An artful manager, that crept between
His friend and shame, and was a kind of screen.
But 'faith, your friends will soon be sore;
Patriots there are, who wish you'd jest no more--
And where's the glory? 'twill be only thought
The Great Man never offered you a groat.
Go, see Sir Robert--P. See Sir Robert!--hum--
And never laugh--for all my life to come?
Seen him I have, but in his happier hour
Of social pleasure, ill-exchanged for power;
Seen him, unencumbered with the venal tribe,
Smile without art, and win without a bribe.
Would he oblige me? let me only find
He does not think me what he thinks mankind.
Come, come, at all I laugh he laughs, no doubt;
The only difference is I dare laugh out.
   F. Why, yes: with Scripture still you may be free;
A horse-laugh, if you please, at honesty:
A joke on Jekyl, or some odd old Whig
Who never changed his principle, or wig:

A patriot is a fool in every age,
Whom all Lord Chamberlains allow the stage:
These nothing hurts; they keep their fashion still,
And wear their strange old virtue, as they will.
If any ask you, "Who's the man, so near
His prince, that writes in verse, and has his ear?"
Why, answer, Lyttelton, and I'll engage
The worthy youth shall ne'er be in a rage;
But were his verses vile, his whisper base,
You'd quickly find him in Lord Fanny's case.
Sejanus, Wolsey, hurt not honest Fleury,
But well may put some statesmen in a fury.

  Laugh, then, at any, but at fools or foes;
These you but anger, and you mend not those.
Laugh at your friends, and, if your friends are sore,
So much the better, you may laugh the more.
To vice and folly to confine the jest,
Sets half the world, God knows, against the rest;
Did not the sneer of more impartial men
At sense and virtue, balance all again.
Judicious wits spread wide the ridicule,
And charitably comfort knave and fool.

  P. Dear sir, forgive the prejudice of youth;
Adieu distinction, satire, warmth, and truth!
Come, harmless characters, that no one hit;
Come, Henley's oratory, Osborne's wit!
The honey dropping from Favonio's tongue,
The flowers of Bubo, and the flow of Y--ng!
The gracious dew of pulpit eloquence,
And all the well-whipped cream of courtly sense,
That first was H--vy's, F---'s next, and then
The S--te's, and then H--vy's once again.
O, come, that easy Ciceronian style,

So Latin, yet so English all the while,
As, though the pride of Middleton and Bland,
All boys may read, and girls may understand!
Then might I sing, without the least offence,
And all I sung should be the nation's sense;
Or teach the melancholy muse to mourn,
Hang the sad verse on Carolina's urn,
And hail her passage to the realms of rest,
All parts performed, and all her children blessed!
So--satire is no more--I feel it die--
No Gazetteer more innocent than I--
And let, a' God's name, every fool and knave
Be graced through life, and flattered in his grave.
  F. Why so? if satire knows its time and place
You still may lash the greatest--in disgrace:
For merit will by turns forsake them all;
Would you know when? exactly when they fall.
But let all satire in all changes spare
Immortal S--k, and grave De--re.
Silent and soft, as saints remove to heaven,
All ties dissolved and every sin forgiven,
These may some gentle ministerial wing
Receive, and place for ever near a king!
There, where no passion, pride, or shame transport,
Lulled with the sweet nepenthe of a Court;
There, where no father's, brother's, friend's disgrace
Once break their rest, or stir them from their place:
But past the sense of human miseries,
All tears are wiped for ever from all eyes;
No cheek is known to blush, no heart to throb,
Save when they lose a question, or a job.
  P. Good Heaven forbid, that I should blast their glory,
Who know how like Whig ministers to Tory,

And, when three sovereigns died, could scarce be vexed,
Considering what a gracious prince was next.
Have I, in silent wonder, seen such things
As pride in slaves, and avarice in kings;
And at a peer, or peeress, shall I fret,
Who starves a sister, or forswears a debt?
Virtue, I grant you, is an empty boast;
But shall the dignity of vice be lost?
Ye gods! shall Cibber's son, without rebuke,
Swear like a lord, or rich out-rake a duke?
A favourite's porter with his master vie,
Be bribed as often, and as often lie?
Shall Ward draw contracts with a statesman's skill?
Or Japhet pocket, like his grace, a will?
Is it for Bond or Peter (paltry things)
To pay their debts, or keep their faith, like kings?
If Blount despatched himself, he played the man,
And so may'st thou, illustrious Passeran!
But shall a printer, weary of his life,
Learn, from their books, to hang himself and wife?
This, this, my friend, I cannot, must not bear;
Vice thus abused, demands a nation's care;
This calls the Church to deprecate our sin,
And hurls the thunder of the laws on gin.
  Let modest Foster, if he will, excel
Ten Metropolitans in preaching well;
A simple Quaker, or a Quaker's wife,
Outdo Llandaff in doctrine--yea in life:
Let humble Allen, with an awkward shame,
Do good by stealth, and blush to find it fame.
Virtue may choose the high or low degree,
'Tis just alike to virtue, and to me;
Dwell in a monk, or light upon a king,

She's still the same, beloved, contented thing.
Vice is undone, if she forgets her birth,
And stoops from angels to the dregs of earth:
But 'tis the Fall degrades her to a w***e;
Let greatness own her, and she's mean no more;
Her birth, her beauty, crowds and courts confess;
Chaste matrons praise her, and grave bishops bless;
In golden chains the willing world she draws,
And hers the Gospel is, and hers the laws,
Mounts the tribunal, lifts her scarlet head,
And sees pale Virtue carted in her stead.
Lo! at the wheels of her triumphal car
Old England's genius, rough with many a scar,
Dragged in the dust! his arms hang idly round,
His flag inverted trails along the ground!
Our youth, all liveried o'er with foreign gold,
Before her dance: behind her crawl the old!
See thronging millions to the Pagod run,
And offer country, parent, wife, or son;
Hear her black trumpet through the land proclaim
That not to be corrupted is the shame.
In soldier, Churchman, patriot, man in power,
'Tis avarice all, ambition is no more!
See, all our nobles begging to be slaves!
See, all our fools aspiring to be knaves!
The wit of cheats, the courage of a w***e,
Are what ten thousand envy and adore;
All, all look up, with reverential awe,
At crimes that 'scape, or triumph o'er the law;
While truth, worth, wisdom, daily they decry--
"Nothing is sacred now but villainy."
　Yet may this verse (if such a verse remain)
Show there was one who held it in disdain.

DIALOGUE II.

    Fr. 'Tis all a libel--Paxton (sir) will say. }
    P. Not yet, my friend! to-morrow 'faith it may }
And for that very cause I print to-day. }
How should I fret to mangle every line,
In reverence to the sins of thirty-nine!
Vice with such giant strides comes on amain,
Invention strives to be before in vain;
Feign what I will, and paint it e'er so strong,
Some rising genius sins up to my song.
    F. Yet none but you by name the guilty lash;
Even Guthry saves half Newgate by a dash.
Spare, then, the person, and expose the vice.
    P. How, sir? not damn the sharper, but the dice?
Come on, then, satire! general, unconfined,
Spread thy broad wing, and souse on all the kind.
Ye statesmen, priests, of one religion all!
Ye tradesmen vile, in army, court, or hall,
Ye reverend atheists--
         F. Scandal! name them! who?
    P. Why that's the thing you bid me not to do.
Who starved a sister, who forswore a debt,
I never named; the town's inquiring yet.
The poisoning dame--
      F. You mean--
     P. I don't.
       F. You do!
    P. See, now I keep the secret, and not you!
The bribing statesman--

F. Hold, too high you go.
P. The bribed elector--
      F. There you stoop too low.
  P. I fain would please you, if I knew with what;
Tell me, which knave is lawful game, which not?
Must great offenders, once escaped the Crown,
Like royal harts, be never more run down?
Admit your law to spare the knight requires,
As beasts of nature may we hunt the squires?
Suppose I censure--you know what I mean--
To save a bishop, may I name a dean?
  F. A dean, sir? no: his fortune is not made;
You hurt a man that's rising in the trade.
  P. If not the tradesman who set up to-day,
Much less the 'prentice who to-morrow may.
Down, down, proud satire! though a realm be spoiled,
Arraign no mightier thief than wretched Wild;
Or, if a court or country's made a job,
Go drench a pickpocket, and join the mob.
  But, sir, I beg you (for the love of vice!)
The matter's weighty, pray consider twice;
Have you less pity for the needy cheat,
The poor and friendless villain, than the great?
Alas! the small discredit of a bribe
Scarce hurts the lawyer, but undoes the scribe.
Then better, sure, it charity becomes
To tax directors, who (thank God!) have plums;
Still better, ministers; or, if the thing
May pinch even there--why lay it on a king.
  F. Stop! stop!
      P. Must satire, then, nor rise nor fall?
Speak out, and bid me blame no rogues at all.
  F. Yes, strike that Wild, I'll justify the blow.

P. Strike? why the man was hanged ten year ago:
Who now that obsolete example fears?
Even Peter trembles only for his ears.
    F. What? always Peter? Peter thinks you mad;
You make men desperate if they once are bad:
Else might he take to virtue some years hence--
    P. As S---k, if he lives, will love the prince.
    F. Strange spleen to S---k!
            P. Do I wrong the man?
God knows, I praise a courtier where I can.
When I confess, there is who feels for fame,
And melts to goodness, need I Scarb'row name?
Please let me own, in Esher's peaceful grove
(Where Kent and Nature vie for Pelham's love),
The scene, the master, opening to my view,
I sit and dream I see my Craggs anew!
    Even in a bishop I can spy desert;
Secker is decent, Rundel has a heart,
Manners with candour are to Benson given,
To Berkeley, every virtue under Heaven.
    But does the Court a worthy man remove?
That instant, I declare, he has my love:
I shun his zenith, court his mild decline;
Thus Somers once, and Halifax, were mine.
Oft, in the clear, still mirror of retreat,
I studied Shrewsbury, the wise and great:
Carleton's calm sense, and Stanhope's noble flame,
Compared, and knew their generous end the same;
How pleasing Atterbury's softer hour!
How shined the soul, unconquered in the tower!
How can I Pulteney, Chesterfield forget,
While Roman spirit charms, and attic wit:
Argyll, the state's whole thunder born to wield,

And shake alike the senate and the field:
Or Wyndham, just to freedom and the throne,
The master of our passions, and his own?
Names, which I long have loved, nor loved in vain,
Ranked with their friends, not numbered with their train;
And if yet higher the proud list should end,
Still let me say: No follower, but a friend.
   Yet think not, friendship only prompts my lays;
I follow Virtue: where she shines, I praise:
Point she to priest or elder, Whig or Tory,
Or round a Quaker's beaver cast a glory.
I never (to my sorrow, I declare)
Dined with the Man of Ross, or my Lord Mayor.
Some in their choice of friends (nay, look not grave)
Have still a secret bias to a knave:
To find an honest man I beat about,
And love him, court him, praise him, in or out.
   F. Then why so few commended?
      P. Not so fierce!
Find you the virtue, and I'll find the verse.
But random praise--the task can ne'er be done;
Each mother asks it for her booby son,
Each widow asks it for the best of men,
For him she weeps, and him she weds again.
Praise cannot stoop, like satire, to the ground;
The number may be hanged, but not be crowned.
Enough for half the greatest of these days
To 'scape my censure, not expect my praise.
And they not rich? what more can they pretend?
Dare they to hope a poet for their friend?
What Richelieu wanted, Louis scarce could gain,
And what young Ammon wished, but wished in vain.
No power the muse's friendship can command;

No power when virtue claims it, can withstand:
To Cato, Virgil paid one honest line;
O let my country's friends illumine mine!
What are you thinking?
　　F. 'Faith, the thought's no sin:
I think your friends are out, and would be in.
　　P. If merely to come in, sir, they go out,
The way they take is strangely round about.
　　F. They too may be corrupted, you'll allow?
　　P. I only call those knaves who are so now.
Is that too little? Come, then, I'll comply--
Spirit of Arnall! aid me while I lie.
Cobham's a coward, Polwarth is a slave,
And Littelton a dark, designing knave,
St. John has ever been a wealthy fool--
But let me add, Sir Robert's mighty dull,
Has never made a friend in private life,
And was, besides, a tyrant to his wife.
　　But pray, when others praise him, do I blame?
Call Verres, Wolsey, any odious name?
Why rail they, then, if but a wreath of mine,
Oh, all-accomplished St. John! deck thy shrine?
　　What? shall each spur-galled hackney of the day,
When Paxton gives him double pots and pay,
Or each new-pensioned sycophant, pretend
To break my windows, if I treat a friend?
Then wisely plead, to me they meant no hurt,
But 'twas my guest at whom they threw the dirt?
Sure, if I spare the minister, no rules
Of honour bind me, not to maul his tools;
Some, if they cannot cut, it may be said
His saws are toothless, and his hatchet's lead.
　　If angered Turenne, once upon a day,

To see a footman kicked that took his pay:
But when he heard the affront the fellow gave,
Knew one a man of honour, one a knave;
The prudent general turned it to a jest,
And begged, he'd take the pains to kick the rest:
Which not at present having time to do--
    F. Hold, sir! for God's sake where's the affront to you?
Against your worship when had S---k writ?
Or P--ge poured forth the torrent of his wit?
Or grant the bard whose distich all commend
(In power a servant, out of power a friend)
To W---le guilty of some venial sin;
What's that to you who ne'er was out nor in?
    The priest whose flattery be-dropt the Crown,
How hurt he you? he only stained the gown.
And how did, pray, the florid youth offend,
Whose speech you took, and gave it to a friend?
    P. 'Faith, it imports not much from whom it came; }
Whoever borrowed, could not be to blame, }
Since the whole house did afterwards the same. }
Let courtly wits to wits afford supply,
As hog to hog in huts of Westphaly;
If one, through Nature's bounty, or his Lord's,
Has what the frugal, dirty soil affords,
From him the next receives it, thick or thin,
As pure a mess almost as it came in;
The blessed benefit, not there confined,
Drops to the third, who nuzzles close behind;
From tail to mouth, they feed and they carouse:
The last full fairly gives it to the House.
    F. This filthy simile, this beastly line,
Quite turns my stomach--
        P. So does flattery mine;

And all your courtly civet-cats can vent,
Perfume to you, to me is excrement.
But hear me further--Japhet, 'tis agreed,
Writ not, and Chartres scarce could write or read,
In all the courts of Pindus guiltless quite;
But pens can forge, my friend, that cannot write;
And must no egg in Japhet's face be thrown
Because the deed he forged was not my own?
Must never patriot, then, declaim at gin,
Unless, good man! he has been fairly in?
No zealous pastor blame a failing spouse
Without a staring reason on his brows?
And each blasphemer quite escape the rod
Because the insult's not on man, but God?
    Ask you what provocation I have had?
The strong antipathy of good to bad.
When truth or virtue an affront endures,
The affront is mine, my friend, and should be yours.
Mine, as a foe professed to false pretence,
Who think a coxcomb's honour like his sense;
Mine, as a friend to every worthy mind
And mine as man, who feel for all mankind.
    F. You're strangely proud.
        P. So proud, I am no slave: }
So impudent I own myself no knave: }
So odd, my country's ruin makes me grave. }
Yes, I am proud; I must be proud to see
Men not afraid of God afraid of me:
Safe from the Bar, the Pulpit, and the Throne,
Yet touched and shamed by ridicule alone.
    O, sacred weapon left for truth's defence,
Sole dread of folly, vice, and insolence!
To all but heaven-directed hands denied

The muse may give thee, but the gods must guide:
Reverent I touch thee! but with honest zeal,
To rouse the watchmen of the public weal;
To virtue's work provoke the tardy hall,
And goad the prelate slumbering in his stall.
Ye tinsel insects whom a Court maintains
That counts your beauties only by your stains,
Spin all your cobwebs o'er the eye of day!
The muse's wing shall brush you all away;
All his Grace preaches, all his Lordship sings,
All that makes saints of queens, and gods of kings.
All, all but truth, drops dead-born from the press,
Like the last gazette or the last address.
    When black ambition stains a public cause,
A monarch's sword when mad vain-glory draws,
Not Waller's wreath can hide the nation's scar
Nor Boileau turn the feather to a star.
    Not so, when diademed with rays divine,
Touched with the flame that breaks from Virtue's shrine,
Her priestless muse forbids the good to die,
And opes the temple of Eternity.
There other trophies deck the truly brave,
Than such as Anstis casts into the grave;
Far other stars than * and * * wear,
And may descend to Mordington from Stair:
(Such as on Hough's unsullied mitre shine,
Or beam, good Digby, from a heart like thine).
Let envy howl, while heaven's whole chorus sings,
And bark at honour not conferred by kings:
Let flattery sickening see the incense rise
Sweet to the world, and grateful to the skies:
Truth guards the poet, sanctifies the line,
And makes immortal, verse as mean as mine.

Yes, the last pen for freedom let me draw,
When truth stands trembling on the edge of law;
Here, last of Britons! let your names be read;
Are none, none living? let me praise the dead,
And for that cause which made your fathers shine
Fall by the votes of their degenerate line.

Fr. Alas! alas! pray end what you began,
And write next winter more essays on man.

The Codes Of Hammurabi And Moses
W. W. Davies

QTY

The discovery of the Hammurabi Code is one of the greatest achievements of archaeology, and is of paramount interest, not only to the student of the Bible, but also to all those interested in ancient history...

Religion   **ISBN:** *1-59462-338-4*   **Pages:132**
MSRP $12.95

The Theory of Moral Sentiments
Adam Smith

QTY

This work from 1749. contains original theories of conscience amd moral judgment and it is the foundation for systemof morals.

Philosophy ISBN: *1-59462-777-0*   **Pages:536**
MSRP $19.95

Jessica's First Prayer
Hesba Stretton

QTY

In a screened and secluded corner of one of the many railway-bridges which span the streets of London there could be seen a few years ago, from five o'clock every morning until half past eight, a tidily set-out coffee-stall, consisting of a trestle and board, upon which stood two large tin cans, with a small fire of charcoal burning under each so as to keep the coffee boiling during the early hours of the morning when the work-people were thronging into the city on their way to their daily toil...

Pages:84

Childrens   ISBN: *1-59462-373-2*   *MSRP $9.95*

My Life and Work
Henry Ford

QTY

Henry Ford revolutionized the world with his implementation of mass production for the Model T automobile. Gain valuable business insight into his life and work with his own auto-biography... "We have only started on our development of our country we have not as yet, with all our talk of wonderful progress, done more than scratch the surface. The progress has been wonderful enough but..."

Pages:300

Biographies/   **ISBN:** *1-59462-198-5*   *MSRP $21.95*

www.bookjungle.com *email: sales@bookjungle.com fax: 630-214-0564 mail: Book Jungle PO Box 2226 Champaign, IL 61825*

The Art of Cross-Examination
Francis Wellman

I presume it is the experience of every author, after his first book is published upon an important subject, to be almost overwhelmed with a wealth of ideas and illustrations which could readily have been included in his book, and which to his own mind, at least, seem to make a second edition inevitable. Such certainly was the case with me; and when the first edition had reached its sixth impression in five months, I rejoiced to learn that it seemed to my publishers that the book had met with a sufficiently favorable reception to justify a second and considerably enlarged edition. ..

Pages:412

Reference   **ISBN:** *1-59462-647-2*   *MSRP $19.95*

On the Duty of Civil Disobedience
Henry David Thoreau

QTY

Thoreau wrote his famous essay, On the Duty of Civil Disobedience, as a protest against an unjust but popular war and the immoral but popular institution of slave-owning. He did more than write—he declined to pay his taxes, and was hauled off to gaol in consequence. Who can say how much this refusal of his hastened the end of the war and of slavery ?

Law   **ISBN:** *1-59462-747-9*   **Pages:48**

MSRP $7.45

Dream Psychology Psychoanalysis for Beginners
Sigmund Freud

QTY

Sigmund Freud, born Sigismund Schlomo Freud (May 6, 1856 - September 23, 1939), was a Jewish-Austrian neurologist and psychiatrist who co-founded the psychoanalytic school of psychology. Freud is best known for his theories of the unconscious mind, especially involving the mechanism of repression; his redefinition of sexual desire as mobile and directed towards a wide variety of objects; and his therapeutic techniques, especially his understanding of transference in the therapeutic relationship and the presumed value of dreams as sources of insight into unconscious desires.

Pages:196

Psychology   **ISBN:** *1-59462-905-6*   *MSRP $15.45*

The Miracle of Right Thought
Orison Swett Marden

QTY

Believe with all of your heart that you will do what you were made to do. When the mind has once formed the habit of holding cheerful, happy, prosperous pictures, it will not be easy to form the opposite habit. It does not matter how improbable or how far away this realization may see, or how dark the prospects may be, if we visualize them as best we can, as vividly as possible, hold tenaciously to them and vigorously struggle to attain them, they will gradually become actualized, realized in the life. But a desire, a longing without endeavor, a yearning abandoned or held indifferently will vanish without realization.

Pages:360

Self Help   **ISBN:** *1-59462-644-8*   *MSRP $25.45*

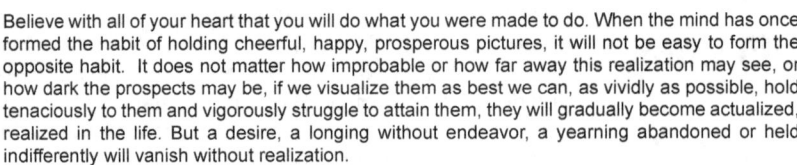

www.bookjungle.com *email: sales@bookjungle.com fax: 630-214-0564 mail: Book Jungle PO Box 2226 Champaign, IL 61825*

QTY

The Rosicrucian Cosmo-Conception Mystic Christianity *by Max Heindel* ISBN: *1-59462-188-8* **$38.95**
The Rosicrucian Cosmo-conception is not dogmatic, neither does it appeal to any other authority than the reason of the student. It is: not controversial, but is: sent forth in the, hope that it may help to clear... *New Age/Religion Pages 646*

Abandonment To Divine Providence *by Jean-Pierre de Caussade* ISBN: *1-59462-228-0* **$25.95**
"The Rev. Jean Pierre de Caussade was one of the most remarkable spiritual writers of the Society of Jesus in France in the 18th Century. His death took place at Toulouse in 1751. His works have gone through many editions and have been republished... *Inspirational/Religion Pages 400*

Mental Chemistry *by Charles Haanel* ISBN: *1-59462-192-6* **$23.95**
Mental Chemistry allows the change of material conditions by combining and appropriately utilizing the power of the mind. Much like applied chemistry creates something new and unique out of careful combinations of chemicals the mastery of mental chemistry... *New Age Pages 354*

The Letters of Robert Browning and Elizabeth Barret Barrett 1845-1846 vol II ISBN: *1-59462-193-4* **$35.95**
by Robert Browning and Elizabeth Barrett *Biographies Pages 596*

Gleanings In Genesis (volume I) *by Arthur W. Pink* ISBN: *1-59462-130-6* **$27.45**
Appropriately has Genesis been termed "the seed plot of the Bible" for in it we have, in germ form, almost all of the great doctrines which are afterwards fully developed in the books of Scripture which follow... *Religion/Inspirational Pages 420*

The Master Key *by L. W. de Laurence* ISBN: *1-59462-001-6* **$30.95**
In no branch of human knowledge has there been a more lively increase of the spirit of research during the past few years than in the study of Psychology, Concentration and Mental Discipline. The requests for authentic lessons in Thought Control, Mental Discipline and... *New Age/Business Pages 422*

The Lesser Key Of Solomon Goetia *by L. W. de Laurence* ISBN: *1-59462-092-X* **$9.95**
This translation of the first book of the "Lemegton" which is now for the first time made accessible to students of Talismanic Magic was done, after careful collation and edition, from numerous Ancient Manuscripts in Hebrew, Latin, and French... *New Age/Occult Pages 92*

Rubaiyat Of Omar Khayyam *by Edward Fitzgerald* ISBN:*1-59462-332-5* **$13.95**
Edward Fitzgerald, whom the world has already learned, in spite of his own efforts to remain within the shadow of anonymity, to look upon as one of the rarest poets of the century, was born at Bredfield, in Suffolk, on the 31st of March, 1809. He was the third son of John Purcell... *Music Pages 172*

Ancient Law *by Henry Maine* ISBN: *1-59462-128-4* **$29.95**
The chief object of the following pages is to indicate some of the earliest ideas of mankind, as they are reflected in Ancient Law, and to point out the relation of those ideas to modern thought. *Religiom/History Pages 452*

Far-Away Stories *by William J. Locke* ISBN: *1-59462-129-2* **$19.45**
"Good wine needs no bush, but a collection of mixed vintages does. And this book is just such a collection. Some of the stories I do not want to remain buried for ever in the museum files of dead magazine-numbers an author's not unpardonable vanity..." *Fiction Pages 272*

Life of David Crockett *by David Crockett* ISBN: *1-59462-250-7* **$27.45**
"Colonel David Crockett was one of the most remarkable men of the times in which he lived. Born in humble life, but gifted with a strong will, an indomitable courage, and unremitting perseverance... *Biographies/New Age Pages 424*

Lip-Reading *by Edward Nitchie* ISBN: *1-59462-206-X* **$25.95**
Edward B. Nitchie, founder of the New York School for the Hard of Hearing, now the Nitchie School of Lip-Reading, Inc, wrote "LIP-READING Principles and Practice". The development and perfecting of this meritorious work on lip-reading was an undertaking... *How-to Pages 400*

A Handbook of Suggestive Therapeutics, Applied Hypnotism, Psychic Science ISBN: *1-59462-214-0* **$24.95**
by Henry Munro *Health/New Age/Health/Self-help Pages 376*

A Doll's House: and Two Other Plays *by Henrik Ibsen* ISBN: *1-59462-112-8* **$19.95**
Henrik Ibsen created this classic when in revolutionary 1848 Rome. Introducing some striking concepts in playwriting for the realist genre, this play has been studied the world over. *Fiction/Classics/Plays 308*

The Light of Asia *by sir Edwin Arnold* ISBN: *1-59462-204-3* **$13.95**
In this poetic masterpiece, Edwin Arnold describes the life and teachings of Buddha. The man who was to become known as Buddha to the world was born as Prince Gautama of India but he rejected the worldly riches and abandoned the reigns of power when... *Religion/History/Biographies Pages 170*

The Complete Works of Guy de Maupassant *by Guy de Maupassant* ISBN: *1-59462-157-8* **$16.95**
"For days and days, nights and nights, I had dreamed of that first kiss which was to consecrate our engagement, and I knew not on what spot I should put my lips..." *Fiction/Classics Pages 240*

The Art of Cross-Examination *by Francis L. Wellman* ISBN: *1-59462-309-0* **$26.95**
Written by a renowned trial lawyer, Wellman imparts his experience and uses case studies to explain how to use psychology to extract desired information through questioning. *How-to/Science/Reference Pages 408*

Answered or Unanswered? *by Louisa Vaughan* ISBN: *1-59462-248-5* **$10.95**
Miracles of Faith in China *Religion Pages 112*

The Edinburgh Lectures on Mental Science (1909) *by Thomas* ISBN: *1-59462-008-3* **$11.95**
This book contains the substance of a course of lectures recently given by the writer in the Queen Street Hall, Edinburgh. Its purpose is to indicate the Natural Principles governing the relation between Mental Action and Material Conditions... *New Age/Psychology Pages 148*

Ayesha *by H. Rider Haggard* ISBN: *1-59462-301-5* **$24.95**
Verily and indeed it is the unexpected that happens! Probably if there was one person upon the earth from whom the Editor of this, and of a certain previous history, did not expect to hear again... *Classics Pages 380*

Ayala's Angel *by Anthony Trollope* ISBN: *1-59462-352-X* **$29.95**
The two girls were both pretty, but Lucy who was twenty-one who supposed to be simple and comparatively unattractive, whereas Ayala was credited, as her Bombwhat romantic name might show, with poetic charm and a taste for romance. Ayala when her father died was nineteen... *Fiction Pages 484*

The American Commonwealth *by James Bryce* ISBN: *1-59462-286-8* **$34.45**
An interpretation of American democratic political theory. It examines political mechanics and society from the perspective of Scotsman James Bryce *Politics Pages 572*

Stories of the Pilgrims *by Margaret P. Pumphrey* ISBN: *1-59462-116-0* **$17.95**
This book explores pilgrims religious oppression in England as well as their escape to Holland and eventual crossing to America on the Mayflower, and their early days in New England... *History Pages 268*

www.bookjungle.com *email: sales@bookjungle.com fax: 630-214-0564 mail: Book Jungle PO Box 2226 Champaign, IL 61825*

QTY

The Fasting Cure *by Sinclair Upton*   ISBN: *1-59462-222-1*   **$13.95**
In the Cosmopolitan Magazine for May, 1910, and in the Contemporary Review (London) for April, 1910, I published an article dealing with my experiences in fasting. I have written a great many magazine articles, but never one which attracted so much attention...   New Age/Self Help/Health Pages 164

Hebrew Astrology *by Sepharial*   ISBN: *1-59462-308-2*   **$13.45**
In these days of advanced thinking it is a matter of common observation that we have left many of the old landmarks behind and that we are now pressing forward to greater heights and to a wider horizon than that which represented the mind-content of our progenitors...   Astrology Pages 144

Thought Vibration or The Law of Attraction in the Thought World   ISBN: *1-59462-127-6*   **$12.95**
by William Walker Atkinson   Psychology/Religion Pages 144

Optimism *by Helen Keller*   ISBN: *1-59462-108-X*   **$15.95**
Helen Keller was blind, deaf, and mute since 19 months old, yet famously learned how to overcome these handicaps, communicate with the world, and spread her lectures promoting optimism. An inspiring read for everyone...   Biographies/Inspirational Pages 84

Sara Crewe *by Frances Burnett*   ISBN: *1-59462-360-0*   **$9.45**
In the first place, Miss Minchin lived in London. Her home was a large, dull, tall one, in a large, dull square, where all the houses were alike, and all the sparrows were alike, and where all the door-knockers made the same heavy sound...   Childrens/Classic Pages 88

The Autobiography of Benjamin Franklin *by Benjamin Franklin*   ISBN: *1-59462-135-7*   **$24.95**
The Autobiography of Benjamin Franklin has probably been more extensively read than any other American historical work, and no other book of its kind has had such ups and downs of fortune. Franklin lived for many years in England, where he was agent...   Biographies/History Pages 332

Name	
Email	
Telephone	
Address	
City, State ZIP	

☐ **Credit Card**   ☐ **Check / Money Order**

Credit Card Number	
Expiration Date	
Signature	

Please Mail to: Book Jungle
PO Box 2226
Champaign, IL 61825
or Fax to: 630-214-0564

ORDERING INFORMATION

web: *www.bookjungle.com*
email: *sales@bookjungle.com*
fax: *630-214-0564*
mail: *Book Jungle PO Box 2226 Champaign, IL 61825*
or PayPal *to sales@bookjungle.com*

Please contact us for bulk discounts

DIRECT-ORDER TERMS

20% Discount if You Order Two or More Books
Free Domestic Shipping!
Accepted: Master Card, Visa, Discover, American Express

www.ingramcontent.com/pod-product-compliance
Lightning Source LLC
Chambersburg PA
CBHW080728020726
47503CB00010B/2837